Front-End Web Development

Techniques and Trends

Kiet Huynh

Table of Contents

Introduction

Welcome to Web Development

In today's digital age, the front-end of a website is often its first impression—a dynamic, engaging interface that captures the user's attention and ensures a seamless browsing experience. The field of front-end web development has evolved dramatically in recent years, pushing the boundaries of what's possible in web design and interactivity. "Front-End Web Development: Techniques and Trends" is your comprehensive guide to mastering this exciting and dynamic discipline.

As the digital landscape continues to shift and user expectations grow, front-end developers play a pivotal role in shaping the online experiences we encounter daily. This book is designed to empower both newcomers and seasoned developers with the knowledge and skills needed to excel in this ever-evolving field.

What This Book Offers:

1. Foundational Knowledge: Whether you're just starting or looking to solidify your understanding, the book begins with the basics. We cover HTML5, CSS3, and JavaScript fundamentals, ensuring you have a strong foundation.

2. Modern Techniques: Stay up-to-date with the latest techniques, including responsive web design, CSS Grid, ES6 JavaScript, and web performance optimization, among others.

3. Frameworks and Libraries: Dive into popular front-end frameworks like React, Angular, and Vue.js. Learn how to build single-page applications (SPAs) and manage state effectively.

4. Web Accessibility: Explore the importance of web accessibility and inclusive design. Understand how to create websites that can be used by everyone, regardless of their abilities.

5. Cross-Browser Compatibility: Overcome the challenges of browser compatibility. Learn strategies for writing code that works smoothly across different browsers and devices.

6. Emerging Trends: Discover the latest trends shaping front-end development, such as Progressive Web Apps (PWAs), serverless architecture, and WebAssembly.

7. Portfolio Building: Learn how to create a professional portfolio, showcase your work, and prepare for interviews and job searches.

8. References and Resources: The book includes handy references on HTML, CSS, JavaScript, and a glossary of key terms.

Who Should Read This Book:

- Aspiring front-end developers looking to break into the field.

- Experienced developers seeking to stay updated on the latest trends and techniques.

- Designers interested in understanding the technical aspects of web development.

- Anyone looking to create modern, accessible, and user-friendly web experiences.

Throughout this book, we emphasize practicality, providing real-world examples and hands-on exercises to reinforce your learning. "Front-End Web Development: Techniques and Trends" is your gateway to becoming a proficient front-end developer who can navigate the ever-changing landscape of web development with confidence. Let's embark on this exciting journey together!

CHAPTER I
Introduction to Front-End Development

1.1 Understanding Front-End vs. Back-End

Front-end and back-end development are the two pillars of web development, each with its unique responsibilities and technologies. In this section, we'll delve into the distinctions between front-end and back-end development and their respective roles in building web applications.

Front-End Development: Shaping User Experiences

Front-end development, often referred to as client-side development, focuses on the user interface and how users interact with a website or web application. It's the visual and interactive part of web development that users see and engage with directly.

Key Responsibilities of Front-End Development:

1. User Interface (UI) Design: Front-end developers collaborate closely with UI/UX designers to create visually appealing and user-friendly interfaces. They translate design mockups into web pages using HTML, CSS, and JavaScript.

2. Interactivity: They make web applications responsive and interactive. This includes handling user input, animations, and ensuring smooth navigation.

3. Cross-Browser Compatibility: Ensuring that web pages work consistently across different web browsers is crucial. Front-end developers tackle browser quirks and compatibility issues.

4. Performance: Optimizing the front-end for speed and efficiency is essential for a seamless user experience. This involves minimizing page load times and optimizing assets like images and scripts.

5. Accessibility: Front-end developers are responsible for making web content accessible to all users, including those with disabilities. They adhere to web accessibility guidelines and implement features like screen reader support.

Back-End Development: Behind-the-Scenes Functionality

While front-end development focuses on what users see and interact with, back-end development handles the behind-the-scenes functionality that powers web applications. It deals with databases, servers, application logic, and server-side scripting.

Key Responsibilities of Back-End Development:

1. Server Configuration: Back-end developers set up and configure servers to host web applications. They choose the appropriate server stack, which may involve technologies like Node.js, Python, Ruby, or PHP.

2. Database Management: Data storage and management are core back-end responsibilities. Developers design and maintain databases, write database queries, and ensure data integrity.

3. Server-Side Logic: The business logic of a web application resides in the back end. Developers write server-side code to handle requests, process data, and generate dynamic content.

4. API Development: Back-end developers often create APIs (Application Programming Interfaces) that allow the front end to communicate with the server. This enables data retrieval and manipulation.

5. Security: Security is a paramount concern. Back-end developers implement security measures to protect data, authenticate users, and safeguard against common web vulnerabilities like SQL injection and cross-site scripting (XSS).

In summary, front-end development focuses on creating user interfaces and ensuring an engaging user experience, while back-end development deals with server-side operations, data management, and application logic. Together, they form a cohesive web development process, with front-end and back-end developers collaborating to build robust and user-friendly web applications. Understanding these distinctions is the first step toward becoming a proficient front-end developer.

1.2 The Role of a Front-End Developer

Front-End developers play a crucial role in shaping the user experience of a website or web application. They are responsible for the visual and interactive elements that users directly interact with. In this section, we'll dive deeper into the role of a front-end developer and explore their key responsibilities.

Understanding the Role

A front-end developer, often referred to as a client-side developer, is essentially the bridge between web designers and back-end developers. Their primary focus is on bringing the design concepts to life and ensuring that the user interface functions seamlessly.

Key Responsibilities of a Front-End Developer:

1. User Interface (UI) Implementation: Front-end developers take the UI/UX design mockups created by web designers and convert them into functional web pages. They use HTML for structuring content, CSS for styling, and JavaScript for interactivity.

2. Cross-Browser Compatibility: Ensuring that a website looks and works consistently across different web browsers (such as Chrome, Firefox, Safari, and Edge) is a fundamental responsibility. Front-end developers need to address browser-specific quirks and ensure compatibility.

3. Responsive Design: With the increasing use of various devices (desktops, laptops, tablets, and smartphones), front-end developers must make websites responsive. This means designing layouts that adapt to different screen sizes and orientations.

4. Interactivity: Front-end developers are responsible for creating interactive features, such as dropdown menus, sliders, forms, and animations, using JavaScript. They handle user input and ensure a smooth and engaging user experience.

5. Performance Optimization: They optimize web pages for performance by minimizing page load times and optimizing assets like images, scripts, and stylesheets. This is crucial for retaining user engagement.

6. Accessibility: Front-end developers ensure that websites are accessible to all users, including those with disabilities. They follow accessibility guidelines (e.g., WCAG) and implement features like alt text for images and proper semantic HTML.

7. Testing and Debugging: Thorough testing is essential to identify and fix issues. Front-end developers perform testing on different devices and browsers, troubleshoot problems, and ensure consistent functionality.

8. Collaboration: They collaborate closely with designers, back-end developers, and other team members to ensure that the final product aligns with the design vision and meets the project's functional requirements.

9. Staying Current: The tech landscape is ever-evolving. Front-end developers stay up-to-date with the latest web technologies, frameworks, and best practices to continuously enhance their skills.

10. Version Control: They often use version control systems like Git to manage code changes collaboratively and track project history.

In summary, front-end developers are responsible for creating visually appealing, user-friendly, and responsive websites or web applications. Their role involves a combination of coding skills, design sensibilities, and a commitment to delivering a positive user experience. They bridge the gap between design and functionality, making them essential contributors to the world of web development.

1.3 Front-End Technologies Overview

In this section, we will provide an overview of the essential front-end technologies that front-end developers use to create captivating and interactive web experiences. Understanding these technologies is crucial for anyone looking to embark on a journey in front-end development.

HTML (Hypertext Markup Language)

HTML serves as the backbone of web content. It provides the structure and semantics necessary to represent web page elements. HTML uses tags to define headings, paragraphs, links, images, forms, and more. Here's a simple example:

```html
<!DOCTYPE html>
<html>
<head>
    <title>Sample Web Page</title>
</head>
<body>
    <h1>Welcome to my website</h1>
    <p>This is a sample paragraph.</p>
    <a href="https://www.example.com">Visit Example.com</a>
</body>
</html>
```

CSS (Cascading Style Sheets)

CSS is responsible for styling the appearance of web pages. It allows developers to control layout, colors, fonts, and other visual aspects. CSS can be applied inline, within HTML, or in external files. Here's a basic CSS example:

```css
/* External CSS file (styles.css) */
body {
    font-family: Arial, sans-serif;
    background-color: #f0f0f0;
}


h1 {
    color: #333;
}
```

JavaScript

JavaScript is a versatile scripting language used to add interactivity and dynamic behavior to web pages. It allows developers to respond to user actions, manipulate the DOM (Document Object Model), and fetch data from servers. Here's a simple JavaScript example:

```javascript
// JavaScript within an HTML document
```

```
function greet() {

  const name = prompt('Enter your name:');

  alert(`Hello, ${name}!`);

}
```
```

## Responsive Web Design

Responsive web design ensures that websites adapt to various screen sizes and devices. It involves using flexible layouts and media queries to make content look and function well on both desktop and mobile devices.

## Front-End Libraries and Frameworks

Front-end developers often leverage libraries and frameworks to streamline development. Popular ones include:

- **React:** Developed by Facebook, React is a JavaScript library for building user interfaces. It allows for the creation of reusable UI components.

- **Angular:** A comprehensive JavaScript framework by Google, Angular simplifies web application development with features like two-way data binding and dependency injection.

- **Vue.js:** Vue is a progressive JavaScript framework for building user interfaces incrementally. It's known for its simplicity and flexibility.

## Build Tools
```

Build tools like Webpack, Gulp, and Grunt automate tasks like bundling JavaScript, compiling CSS, and optimizing assets, making development more efficient.

Version Control

Version control systems like Git help developers track changes, collaborate with others, and manage codebase versions effectively.

Package Managers

Package managers like npm (Node Package Manager) and Yarn simplify the installation and management of libraries, frameworks, and dependencies.

Web Development Browsers

Browsers like Google Chrome, Mozilla Firefox, and Microsoft Edge offer developer tools that aid in debugging and testing web applications.

Conclusion

Front-end development is an exciting field that combines creativity and technology. Understanding these core front-end technologies is the first step towards becoming a proficient front-end developer. As you delve deeper into these technologies, you'll gain the skills necessary to create engaging and responsive web experiences. Whether you're interested in design, interactivity, or user experience, front-end development offers a wealth of opportunities to explore.

CHAPTER II
Setting Up Your Development Environment

2.1 Choosing a Code Editor

Choosing the right code editor is a crucial decision for any developer. It's the tool where you'll spend most of your time writing, testing, and debugging code. In this section, we'll explore the factors to consider when selecting a code editor and provide recommendations for some popular options.

Factors to Consider

Before diving into specific code editors, let's consider the factors that should influence your decision:

1. Ease of Use: A good code editor should be user-friendly and offer a smooth writing experience. Look for features like syntax highlighting, auto-completion, and a customizable interface.

2. Language Support: Ensure that the code editor supports the programming languages and technologies you'll be working with. Most editors are versatile, but some may excel in specific areas.

3. Extensibility: Extensibility is a significant advantage. Editors with a rich ecosystem of plugins and extensions allow you to tailor your development environment to your needs.

4. Cross-Platform: If you work on different operating systems, consider a code editor that is available on multiple platforms, such as Windows, macOS, and Linux.

5. Performance: A snappy and responsive code editor can significantly improve your productivity. Avoid editors that suffer from lag or resource-heavy performance.

6. Community and Support: A strong and active user community often results in better support, a wealth of resources, and regular updates.

Popular Code Editors

Here are some well-regarded code editors, each with its unique strengths:

1. Visual Studio Code (VS Code):

   - Developed by Microsoft, VS Code is a highly extensible and versatile code editor.

   - It supports a wide range of languages and offers a massive library of extensions.

   - Features like IntelliSense, Git integration, and a built-in terminal make it a favorite among developers.

2. Sublime Text:

   - Known for its speed and minimalistic design, Sublime Text is an elegant choice.

   - It supports multiple programming languages and boasts a vast package ecosystem.

   - Sublime Text's "Goto Anything" feature simplifies navigation in large projects.

3. Atom:

- Atom is an open-source code editor created by GitHub.

- It is highly customizable, and you can create your packages using web technologies.

- Collaboration is easy with features like Teletype for real-time coding with others.

4. Visual Studio:

- If you're working with .NET or C#, Visual Studio is a powerful integrated development environment (IDE) by Microsoft.

- It offers comprehensive tools for web and desktop application development.

5. Eclipse:

- Eclipse is an open-source IDE known for its robust support for Java development.

- It has a vast ecosystem of plugins for other programming languages and technologies.

Conclusion

Choosing the right code editor is a personal decision that depends on your preferences and the specific needs of your projects. It's worth trying out a few options to see which one aligns best with your workflow and style. Remember that your choice of code editor is just one part of your development environment, but it can significantly impact your coding experience and productivity.

2.2 Installing and Configuring Development Tools

In this section, we'll guide you through the process of installing and configuring essential development tools. A well-configured development environment is crucial for a smooth workflow, efficient coding, and effective debugging. We'll cover the setup of a basic development environment on Windows, macOS, or Linux.

1. Installing Node.js and npm

Node.js is a JavaScript runtime that allows you to execute JavaScript code outside of a web browser. It's commonly used for server-side scripting and building JavaScript-based applications. npm (Node Package Manager) is a package manager for Node.js libraries and tools.

Steps:

- **Windows:**

  - Download the Windows Installer for Node.js from the official website.

  - Run the installer, follow the prompts, and ensure that both Node.js and npm are installed.

  - To verify the installation, open your command prompt and run `node -v` and `npm -v` to check the versions.

- **macOS:**

  - You can install Node.js and npm on macOS using Homebrew, a package manager for macOS.

  - Open Terminal and run the following commands:

    - Install Homebrew: `/bin/bash -c "$(curl -fsSL https://raw.githubusercontent.com/Homebrew/install/HEAD/install.sh)"`

    - Install Node.js and npm: `brew install node`

- To verify the installation, run `node -v` and `npm -v` in Terminal.

- Linux (Ubuntu/Debian):

  - Use the package manager to install Node.js and npm:

    - `sudo apt-get update`

    - `sudo apt-get install nodejs npm`

  - Verify the installation with `node -v` and `npm -v`.

2. Setting Up Git

Git is a distributed version control system that tracks changes in your codebase and enables collaboration with others. It's an essential tool for managing your project's source code.

Steps:

- Windows:

  - Download the Git for Windows installer from the official website.

  - Run the installer and follow the installation steps.

  - Open Git Bash (installed with Git) to access the command-line interface.

- macOS:

  - On macOS, Git is usually pre-installed. You can open Terminal and run `git --version` to check if it's available.

  - If not installed, you can download the macOS Git installer from the official website and follow the installation steps.

- **Linux (Ubuntu/Debian):**

  - Install Git using the package manager:

    - `sudo apt-get update`

    - `sudo apt-get install git`

  - Verify the installation with `git --version`.

3. Code Editor Setup

Refer to the previous section on choosing a code editor to select and install your preferred code editor.

4. Additional Development Tools

Depending on your specific development needs, you may want to install additional tools such as database management systems, web servers, or text editors for various file types. Make sure to choose tools that align with your project requirements.

Conclusion

Setting up your development environment is a critical first step in your journey as a front-end developer. A well-configured environment with the right tools will enhance your productivity and help you build high-quality web applications. In the next section, we'll dive into the essentials of version control with Git, which is vital for managing your codebase and collaborating with others.

2.3 Version Control with Git

In this section, we'll dive into the world of version control using Git. Git is an essential tool for tracking changes in your codebase, collaborating with others, and ensuring the integrity of your project. We'll cover the basics of Git and provide step-by-step instructions on how to get started.

1. Installing Git

Before you can use Git, you need to install it on your computer if it's not already installed. Follow these installation steps based on your operating system:

- Windows:

  - Download the Git for Windows installer from the official website.

  - Run the installer and follow the installation steps.

  - During installation, you'll have several options to configure Git, including your preferred text editor and line ending conversions. You can choose the default settings for now.

  - Once installed, open Git Bash, a command-line interface for Git.

- macOS:

  - On macOS, Git is often pre-installed. Open Terminal and run `git --version` to check if it's available.

  - If Git is not installed, you can download the macOS Git installer from the official website and follow the installation steps.

- Linux (Ubuntu/Debian):

  - Install Git using the package manager:

    - `sudo apt-get update`

- `sudo apt-get install git`

- Verify the installation with `git --version`.

2. Configuration

After installing Git, you should configure it with your name and email address. This information is used to identify your commits.

Open your command-line interface (Git Bash, Terminal, or another terminal) and run the following commands:

```bash
git config --global user.name "Your Name"
git config --global user.email "your.email@example.com"
```

Replace "Your Name" and "your.email@example.com" with your name and email address. These settings will be used for all your Git repositories.

3. Creating a Git Repository

A Git repository, or repo, is a place where your project's source code and history are stored. To create a new Git repository for your project, follow these steps:

- Navigate to your project's directory using the command line.

- Run the following command to initialize a new Git repository:

```bash
git init
```

This command creates a hidden directory called `.git` in your project folder, where Git stores its data.

4. Staging and Committing Changes

Git uses a staging area to track changes before they are committed to the repository. To commit your changes, follow these steps:

- Use the following command to stage your changes:

```bash
git add .
```

This command stages all changes in your project directory.

- To commit the staged changes, run:

```bash
git commit -m "Your commit message here"
```

```
```

Replace "Your commit message here" with a brief description of the changes you made.

5. Viewing Repository History

To view the history of commits in your Git repository, use the following command:

```bash
git log
```

This command displays a list of commits, including their unique identifiers (hashes), authors, dates, and commit messages.

6. Working with Remote Repositories

Git allows you to collaborate with others by pushing and pulling changes from remote repositories hosted on platforms like GitHub, GitLab, or Bitbucket. To work with remote repositories, you'll need to add remote repositories and perform operations like push and pull.

Note: This section provides an overview of Git's essential features. We'll explore Git in more detail, including branching, merging, and collaborating on projects.

Conclusion

Git is a powerful version control system that is fundamental to modern software development. In this section, we've covered the basics of installing Git, configuring it, creating a Git repository, staging and committing changes, viewing the commit history, and introduced the concept of remote repositories. With these fundamental Git skills, you'll be well-prepared for effective version control in your front-end development projects.

CHAPTER III
HTML5 Essentials

3.1 HTML Document Structure

HTML (Hypertext Markup Language) serves as the backbone of web content. It provides the structure and semantics that web browsers use to render web pages. In this chapter, we'll dive into the essentials of HTML5 document structure, which lays the foundation for building web content. Understanding HTML structure is crucial because it forms the basis for creating web pages that are well-organized, semantically meaningful, and accessible.

Basic Document Structure

An HTML document is structured using elements, which are enclosed in tags. A typical HTML5 document begins with a `<!DOCTYPE>` declaration to specify the version of HTML being used, followed by an opening and closing `<html>` tag. Within the `<html>` tag, there are two main sections: `<head>` and `<body>`.

```html
<!DOCTYPE html>
<html>
  <head>
    <!-- Metadata and links to external resources go here -->
    <title>Document Title</title>
    <meta charset="UTF-8">
```

```
    <link rel="stylesheet" href="styles.css">
  </head>
  <body>
    <!-- Content visible to users goes here -->
    <h1>Welcome to My Web Page</h1>
    <p>This is a simple HTML document.</p>
  </body>
</html>
```

1. `<!DOCTYPE html>`: This declaration tells the browser that the document is written in HTML5.

2. `<html>`: The root element of an HTML document that contains all other elements.

3. `<head>`: Contains metadata and links to external resources like stylesheets, scripts, and character encodings.

4. `<body>`: Contains the visible content that users interact with on the web page.

Document Metadata

Inside the `<head>` section, you can include important metadata about your document. Some commonly used metadata elements include:

- `<title>`: Sets the title of the web page, which is displayed in the browser's title bar or tab.

- `<meta charset="UTF-8">`: Specifies the character encoding of the document. UTF-8 is a widely used encoding that supports a vast range of characters.

- `<link>`: Used to link external resources like stylesheets (CSS) to the HTML document.

Semantic HTML Elements

HTML5 introduces a range of semantic elements that describe the meaning of content rather than just specifying how it should be presented. Using semantic elements makes your HTML more accessible and SEO-friendly. Some important semantic elements include:

- `<header>`: Represents a container for introductory content, often containing a logo, site title, or navigation menu.

- `<nav>`: Represents a section of navigation links, such as a menu.

- `<main>`: Contains the primary content of a document. There should be only one `<main>` element per page.

- `<section>`: Defines a section of content within an HTML document. It's often used to group related content together.

- `<article>`: Represents a self-contained composition in a document, such as a blog post or news article.

- `<aside>`: Represents content that is tangentially related to the content around it, like a sidebar or advertising.

- `**<footer>**`: Contains metadata or information about the containing section or document.

Forms and Input Validation

HTML5 provides enhanced support for creating forms, which are essential for collecting user input. You can use elements like `<form>`, `<input>`, `<textarea>`, and `<button>` to create forms. HTML5 also introduces input types like `email`, `url`, `number`, and `date`, which provide better validation and user experience.

Here's an example of a simple form:

```html
<form action="/submit" method="post">
  <label for="name">Name:</label>
  <input type="text" id="name" name="name" required>

  <label for="email">Email:</label>
  <input type="email" id="email" name="email" required>

  <button type="submit">Submit</button>
</form>
```

- `**<form>**`: Defines a form that collects user input.

- `<label>`: Provides a label for an input element, improving accessibility and usability.

- `<input>`: Represents an input control. The `type` attribute specifies the input type, and `required` enforces field completion.

- `<button>`: Represents a clickable button, often used for form submission.

HTML5 also introduced attributes like `min`, `max`, `pattern`, and `placeholder` to help with input validation and user guidance.

HTML5 Media Elements

HTML5 includes built-in support for embedding multimedia content like audio and video. The `<audio>` and `<video>` elements allow you to include audio and video files directly in your web pages, reducing the reliance on third-party plugins like Flash.

```html
<audio controls>
  <source src="song.mp3" type="audio/mpeg">
  Your browser does not support the audio element.
</audio>


<video controls width="640" height="360">
  <source src="video.mp4" type="video/mp4">
  Your browser does not support the video element.
</video>
```

```
```

- `**<audio>**`: Embeds audio content, and the `controls` attribute adds audio player controls.

- `**<video>**`: Embeds video content, and the `controls` attribute adds video player controls. The `width` and `height` attributes specify the dimensions.

- `**<source>**`: Defines multiple media resources for the browser to choose from, based on its capabilities. It specifies the source URL and media type.

By understanding the HTML5 document structure, semantic elements, form creation, and media embedding, you're equipped to create well-structured and feature-rich web pages. HTML is the foundation of web development, and mastering it is essential for building robust and accessible websites. In the following chapters, we'll explore these topics in greater detail, diving deeper into HTML5, CSS, and JavaScript to empower you with the skills to create compelling web experiences.

3.2 Semantic HTML Elements

Semantic HTML elements are an essential aspect of modern web development. They provide a way to structure your web content in a meaningful and organized manner. By using semantic elements, you make it easier for both browsers and developers to understand the structure and purpose of your web page. This section will delve into some of the most commonly used semantic elements in HTML5 and explain how to use them effectively.

1. `<header>` - Defining Page Headers

The `<header>` element is used to represent introductory content or a set of navigational links. It's typically placed at the top of a web page and contains elements such as a logo, site title, and main navigation menu. Here's an example of a simple header:

```html
<header>
  <h1>My Website</h1>
  <nav>
    <ul>
      <li><a href="/">Home</a></li>
      <li><a href="/about">About</a></li>
      <li><a href="/contact">Contact</a></li>
    </ul>
  </nav>
</header>
```

In this example, we have a `<header>` element containing an `<h1>` heading for the site's title and a `<nav>` element for the navigation menu.

2. `<nav>` - Navigation Menus

The `<nav>` element is specifically used to define navigation menus, such as site navigation or menus within a page. It helps screen readers and search engines identify the content's navigational structure. Here's how you can use it:

```html
<nav>
 <ul>
   <li><a href="/">Home</a></li>
   <li><a href="/about">About</a></li>
   <li><a href="/contact">Contact</a></li>
 </ul>
</nav>
```

The `<nav>` element is typically placed within the `<header>` or `<footer>` of a web page.

3. `<main>` - Main Content Area

The `<main>` element represents the primary content of a web page. There should be only one `<main>` element per page, and it should contain the most relevant content. Here's an example:

```html
<main>
 <h1>Welcome to My Blog</h1>
 <article>
  <h2>Article Title</h2>
  <p>Article content goes here...</p>
 </article>
</main>
```

The `<main>` element is a crucial part of creating accessible web pages because it helps screen readers identify the main content.

4. `<article>` - Self-Contained Content

The `<article>` element is used to represent a self-contained composition in a document, such as a blog post, news article, or forum post. It should make sense on its own and be distributable independently from the rest of the content. Here's an example:

```html
<article>
 <h2>How to Bake the Perfect Apple Pie</h2>
 <p>Instructions and ingredients...</p>
</article>
```

By using `<article>`, you convey that the content within it is a stand-alone piece.

5. `<section>` - Grouping Content

The `<section>` element defines a section within an HTML document and is often used to group related content. It doesn't carry any specific semantic meaning on its own but helps structure content. For example:

```html
<section>
  <h2>Web Development Tools</h2>
  <p>Information about web development tools...</p>
</section>
```

`<section>` elements are useful for organizing content and can be nested to create a hierarchical structure.

6. `<aside>` - Tangentially Related Content

The `<aside>` element represents content that is tangentially related to the content around it. It's often used for sidebars, pull quotes, or advertising. Here's an example:

```html
<article>
  <h2>Web Design Tips</h2>
```

```
  <p>Article content...</p>
  <aside>
   <h3>Related Links</h3>
   <ul>
    <li><a href="#">Learn more about web design</a></li>
    <li><a href="#">Web design courses</a></li>
   </ul>
  </aside>
</article>
```

`<aside>` helps identify content that is not the main focus but provides additional context.

7. `<footer>` - Document or Section Footer

The `<footer>` element represents the footer of a section or the entire document. It often contains metadata, copyright information, or links to related documents. Here's an example:

```html
<footer>
  <p>&copy; 2023 My Website</p>
  <p><a href="/privacy">Privacy Policy</a> | <a href="/terms">Terms of Service</a></p>
</footer>
```

Including a `<footer>` element in your document improves its structure and accessibility.

By incorporating these semantic HTML elements into your web pages, you not only improve the structure and clarity of your content but also make it more accessible to users with disabilities and more search engine-friendly. Semantic HTML is a fundamental building block of modern web development, helping you create well-organized and meaningful web pages. In the next sections of this chapter, we'll explore forms and input validation as well as HTML5 media elements.

3.3 Forms and Input Validation

Forms are an integral part of web development, allowing users to submit data to a server. HTML5 introduced several new form elements and attributes that enhance the user experience and simplify data validation. In this section, we'll explore how to create forms and perform input validation using HTML5.

Creating a Simple Form

To create a basic form in HTML5, you can use the `<form>` element along with various input elements like `<input>`, `<textarea>`, and `<button>`. Let's create a simple contact form:

```html
<form action="/submit" method="post">
  <label for="name">Name:</label>
  <input type="text" id="name" name="name" required>

  <label for="email">Email:</label>
  <input type="email" id="email" name="email" required>

  <label for="message">Message:</label>
  <textarea id="message" name="message" rows="4" required></textarea>

  <button type="submit">Submit</button>
</form>
```

In this example, we've used the `<form>` element to create a form that will be submitted to the "/submit" URL using the HTTP POST method. Each input field is labeled using the `<label>` element, and the `for` attribute is used to associate labels with input fields.

The `required` attribute is added to each input element to specify that the fields must be filled out before the form can be submitted.

Input Types and Attributes

HTML5 introduced various input types and attributes that enhance user interactions and input validation.

- `<input type="email">`: This input type is used for email addresses and automatically validates whether the input is a valid email address.

- `<input type="url">`: This input type is used for URLs (web addresses) and validates URL formats.

- `<input type="number">`: This input type is used for numeric input and can have attributes like `min` and `max` to specify acceptable value ranges.

- `<input type="date">`, `<input type="time">`, and `<input type="datetime-local">`: These input types allow users to pick dates and times from a calendar or input them manually.

- `<input type="checkbox">` and `<input type="radio">`: These input types are used for checkboxes and radio buttons, respectively, to select options.

- `<input type="file">`: This input type lets users upload files. The `accept` attribute can specify allowed file types.

Input Validation

HTML5 provides built-in validation for various input types. For example, using `<input type="email">` will automatically check if the input is a valid email address. Similarly, `<input type="number">` will ensure that users enter a numeric value within the specified range.

Custom validation messages can be provided using the `pattern` attribute and regular expressions. For instance, to validate a phone number format, you can use:

```html
<input type="text" id="phone" name="phone" pattern="[0-9]{10}" title="Enter a 10-digit phone number">
```

In this example, the `pattern` attribute specifies that the input should consist of exactly 10 digits, and the `title` attribute provides a custom error message if the input doesn't match the pattern.

Using JavaScript for Validation

While HTML5 provides basic form validation, more complex validation logic may require JavaScript. You can use JavaScript event handlers like `onsubmit` to trigger custom validation functions before the form is submitted.

Here's a simple example of using JavaScript to validate a form:

```html
<script>
  function validateForm() {
    var name = document.forms["myForm"]["name"].value;
    if (name == "") {
      alert("Name must be filled out");
      return false;
    }
    // Add more validation logic here
  }
</script>


<form name="myForm" action="/submit" method="post" onsubmit="return validateForm()">
  <!-- Form fields -->
  <button type="submit">Submit</button>
</form>
```

In this example, the `validateForm` JavaScript function is called when the form is submitted. It checks if the name field is empty and displays an alert if validation fails.

By combining HTML5's built-in validation features with JavaScript, you can create powerful and user-friendly forms on your website. Ensure that your forms provide clear feedback to users and prevent invalid submissions as much as possible.

In the next section, we'll explore HTML5 media elements and how to embed audio and video in your web pages.

3.4 HTML5 Media Elements

HTML5 introduced several media elements that allow web developers to easily embed audio and video content into web pages. In this section, we'll explore the HTML5 `<audio>` and `<video>` elements and learn how to use them effectively.

Embedding Audio with `<audio>` Element

The `<audio>` element is used to embed audio content, such as music or sound effects, directly into a web page. Let's create a simple example of how to use it:

```html
<audio controls>
  <source src="audio.mp3" type="audio/mpeg">
  Your browser does not support the audio element.
</audio>
```

In this example:

- The `controls` attribute adds audio playback controls (play, pause, volume, etc.) to the audio player.

- The `<source>` element specifies the audio file to be played (`audio.mp3`) and its MIME type (`type`). You can provide multiple `<source>` elements with different file formats (e.g., MP3, Ogg, WAV) to ensure cross-browser compatibility.

- The text inside the `<audio>` element ("Your browser does not support the audio element.") is displayed if the browser doesn't support the `<audio>` element or any of the specified source formats.

Embedding Video with `<video>` Element

The `<video>` element is used to embed video content into web pages. Here's a basic example:

```html
<video controls width="640" height="360">
  <source src="video.mp4" type="video/mp4">
  Your browser does not support the video element.
</video>
```

In this example:

- The `controls` attribute adds video playback controls to the video player.

- The `width` and `height` attributes set the dimensions of the video player.

- Like with the `<audio>` element, the `<source>` element specifies the video file to be played (`video.mp4`) and its MIME type (`type`). You can provide multiple source elements for different formats.

- The text inside the `<video>` element is displayed if the browser doesn't support the `<video>` element or any of the specified source formats.

Fallback Content

Including fallback content (text or other HTML elements) inside the `<audio>` and `<video>` elements is essential. It ensures that users with browsers that don't support these elements or the specified formats can still access the content.

Autoplay and Looping

You can use the `autoplay` attribute to make media content start playing automatically when the page loads. However, be cautious with this feature, as it can be disruptive to users and may not be allowed in certain situations (e.g., autoplay with sound).

To loop audio or video playback, use the `loop` attribute. This causes the media to play continuously until the user stops it.

Accessibility and Captions

For accessibility, it's crucial to provide closed captions or subtitles for audio and video content. You can do this by including the `<track>` element within the media element:

```html
<video controls>
  <source src="video.mp4" type="video/mp4">
  <track label="English" kind="subtitles" src="captions.vtt" srclang="en" default>
  Your browser does not support the video element.
</video>
```

```
```

In this example, the `<track>` element specifies a captions file (`captions.vtt`) and the language (`en` for English). The `kind` attribute indicates that it's subtitles. The `default` attribute makes it the default captions track.

Customizing the Media Player

You can style the appearance of the media player controls using CSS. Additionally, JavaScript can be used to control media playback programmatically, allowing for custom functionality and interactions.

HTML5 media elements provide a powerful way to incorporate audio and video content into your web pages, enhancing user engagement and interactivity. When using media elements, consider accessibility, compatibility, and user experience to ensure a seamless multimedia experience for all visitors to your site.

CHAPTER IV
Mastering CSS3

4.1 Styling with CSS

Cascading Style Sheets (CSS) is a fundamental technology in web development that allows you to control the presentation and layout of your HTML content. In this section, we will explore the basics of styling with CSS, covering the essential concepts and techniques.

Introduction to CSS

CSS is used to define the visual style and layout of web documents. It enables you to control various aspects of your webpage, such as colors, fonts, spacing, and positioning. CSS separates the content (HTML) from its presentation, making it easier to maintain and update your website's design.

Linking CSS to HTML

To apply CSS to an HTML document, you need to link the CSS file to your HTML file using the `<link>` element in the document's `<head>` section. Here's an example of how to link an external CSS file:

```html
<!DOCTYPE html>
<html>
```

```
<head>
  <link rel="stylesheet" type="text/css" href="styles.css">
</head>
<body>
  <!-- Your HTML content goes here -->
</body>
</html>
```

In this example, the `href` attribute in the `<link>` element specifies the path to the external CSS file (`styles.css`). This file contains your CSS rules.

CSS Selectors

Selectors are used to target HTML elements that you want to style. There are various types of selectors, including:

- **Element Selectors:** Target elements based on their HTML tag names, e.g., `p` for paragraphs or `h1` for headings.

- **Class Selectors:** Target elements with a specific `class` attribute, e.g., `.highlight` selects all elements with `class="highlight"`.

- **ID Selectors:** Target a single element with a specific `id` attribute, e.g., `#header` selects the element with `id="header"`.

- **Descendant Selectors:** Select elements that are descendants of another element, e.g., `ul li` selects all `li` elements within a `ul`.

- **Pseudo-classes and Pseudo-elements:** Apply styles to elements based on their state or position in the document, e.g., `:hover` for hover states or `::before` for pseudo-elements.

CSS Properties and Values

CSS properties define the aspects of an element that you want to style, and values specify how you want to style them. Here are some common CSS properties and their values:

- `color`: Sets the text color, e.g., `color: blue;`.

- `font-size`: Defines the size of the text, e.g., `font-size: 16px;`.

- `background-color`: Sets the background color, e.g., `background-color: #f0f0f0;`.

- `margin` and `padding`: Control spacing around elements, e.g., `margin: 10px; padding: 20px;`.

- `border`: Defines borders around elements, e.g., `border: 1px solid #ccc;`.

- `width` and `height`: Set the dimensions of elements, e.g., `width: 300px; height: 200px;`.

Creating CSS Rules

CSS rules consist of selectors and declarations. Declarations include one or more property-value pairs enclosed in curly braces `{}`. Here's a simple CSS rule:

```css
p {
  color: red;
  font-size: 18px;
}
```

In this example, the `p` selector targets all `<p>` elements, and the declarations set the text color and font size.

Inline CSS vs. Internal CSS vs. External CSS

- **Inline CSS:** You can apply CSS directly to individual HTML elements using the `style` attribute, but it's not recommended for large-scale styling due to maintenance issues.

- **Internal CSS:** You can place CSS rules within a `<style>` element in the HTML document's `<head>` section. This approach is suitable for small projects or when you want to isolate CSS styles for a specific document.

- **External CSS:** As shown earlier, you can link an external CSS file to your HTML document. This is the most scalable and maintainable way to apply styles, especially when working on multiple web pages.

CSS Box Model

Understanding the CSS box model is crucial for controlling the layout and spacing of elements. The box model consists of the content area, padding, border, and margin. You can manipulate each part to control an element's size and spacing.

Conclusion

Styling with CSS is an essential skill for web developers. It allows you to create visually appealing and responsive web designs. By using CSS selectors, properties, and values effectively, you can control the presentation of your HTML content. In the next sections, we will delve deeper into CSS layout techniques, responsive design, and advanced CSS features like CSS Grid and Flexbox.

4.2 CSS Layout Techniques

CSS Layout Techniques

In this section, we will explore CSS layout techniques that are essential for creating well-structured and responsive web designs. Understanding how to control the positioning and arrangement of elements on a webpage is crucial for web developers.

1. The CSS Box Model

Before diving into layout techniques, it's essential to understand the CSS box model, which defines how elements are rendered in terms of content, padding, border, and margin. Each of these components contributes to the overall size and spacing of an element.

Here's a brief overview:

- **Content:** This is the actual area where the element's content, like text or images, is displayed.

- **Padding:** Padding is the space between the content and the element's border. You can control it using the `padding` property.

- **Border:** The border surrounds the padding and content. You can define the border using the `border` property.

- **Margin:** The margin is the space outside the border that separates an element from its neighboring elements. You can set margins with the `margin` property.

Understanding how these components interact helps you control the layout more effectively.

2. Display Property

The `display` property controls how an element is displayed on the webpage. Common values include:

- `block`: Makes an element a block-level element, which means it takes up the full width available and starts on a new line. Example: `<div>`.

- `inline`: Makes an element an inline-level element, allowing it to flow within text content. Example: `<span>`.

- `inline-block`: Combines properties of both block and inline elements, allowing elements to flow with text content while still being able to set width and height. Useful for creating inline elements with defined dimensions.

3. Position Property

The `position` property defines how an element is positioned within its containing element. Common values include:

- `static` (default): Elements are positioned in the normal flow of the document.

- `relative`: Elements are positioned relative to their normal position in the document flow. You can use properties like `top`, `right`, `bottom`, and `left` to offset them.

- `absolute`: Elements are removed from the normal document flow and positioned relative to the nearest positioned ancestor. If no positioned ancestor exists, it's positioned relative to the initial containing block.

- `fixed`: Elements are removed from the normal document flow and positioned relative to the viewport. They stay fixed even when the page is scrolled.

4. Floats

The `float` property allows you to push an element to one side (left or right) and make other elements flow around it. This technique was commonly used for creating multi-column layouts before the advent of CSS Grid and Flexbox.

```css
.example {
  float: left;
  width: 50%;
}
```

5. Clear Property

When working with floated elements, you may need to use the `clear` property to ensure that elements don't wrap around a floated element. Common values are `left`, `right`, and `both`.

```css
.clearfix::after {
```

```
  content: "";

  display: table;

  clear: both;

}
```
```

## 6. CSS Positioning Techniques

CSS positioning techniques, such as creating sticky headers or footers, can be achieved using the `position: sticky` property and `position: fixed`. These techniques are useful for creating navigational menus or elements that remain visible as users scroll down the page.

## Conclusion

Mastering CSS layout techniques is fundamental for web development. Understanding the CSS box model, the `display` property, `position` property, floats, and clears will enable you to create complex and responsive web layouts. In the following sections, we'll explore more advanced layout methods like CSS Grid and Flexbox, as well as responsive web design principles.
```

4.3 CSS Grid and Flexbox

CSS Grid and Flexbox are two powerful layout techniques introduced in CSS3 that make designing complex layouts more accessible and efficient. They provide web developers with precise control over the arrangement and alignment of elements within a webpage. In this section, we'll explore both CSS Grid and Flexbox in detail and provide practical examples for better understanding.

1. CSS Grid Layout

CSS Grid Layout, often referred to as just Grid, is a two-dimensional layout system that allows you to create grid structures for complex layouts. It's ideal for creating both rows and columns in your design, making it well-suited for grid-based designs. Here's how to get started:

Defining the Grid Container:

To create a grid layout, you first define a grid container using the `display: grid;` property. For example:

```css
.grid-container {
  display: grid;
  grid-template-columns: 1fr 1fr 1fr; /* Three equal-width columns */
  grid-gap: 10px; /* Gap between grid items */
}
```

Placing Grid Items:

Inside the grid container, you can place grid items by specifying their location using `grid-row` and `grid-column` properties or using shorthand like `grid-area`. For instance:

```css
.grid-item {
  grid-row: 2 / 3; /* Places the item in the second row */
  grid-column: 2 / 4; /* Places the item from the second to the fourth column */
}
```

2. CSS Flexbox Layout

Flexbox, or the Flexible Box Layout, is a one-dimensional layout system that excels at distributing space along a single axis (either horizontally or vertically). It's perfect for creating flexible and responsive layouts. Here's how to use it:

Defining the Flex Container:

To create a flex layout, you define a flex container using the `display: flex;` property. For example:

```css
.flex-container {
  display: flex;
```

```
flex-direction: row; /* Items flow horizontally */

justify-content: space-between; /* Items spaced equally along the main axis */

align-items: center; /* Items vertically centered */

}
```

Placing Flex Items:

Inside the flex container, you place flex items. These items automatically adjust their size to fill the available space. For instance:

```css
.flex-item {

  flex: 1; /* Each item equally shares available space */

}
```

3. CSS Grid vs. Flexbox

Understanding when to use CSS Grid or Flexbox is essential:

- **CSS Grid** is ideal for creating complex two-dimensional layouts with both rows and columns. It's well-suited for grid-based designs and aligning items in both directions.

- **Flexbox** is best for one-dimensional layouts and distributing space along a single axis. It's great for aligning items either horizontally or vertically but doesn't handle two-dimensional grids as effectively as CSS Grid.

Practical Examples:

1. Creating a Grid-Based Gallery: Show how to use CSS Grid to create a responsive image gallery.

2. Building a Flexible Navigation Bar: Demonstrate using Flexbox for creating a responsive navigation bar that adapts to different screen sizes.

3. Combining Grid and Flexbox: Showcase a complex layout that combines both Grid and Flexbox to achieve a unique design.

Conclusion

CSS Grid and Flexbox are essential tools for modern web layout design. By mastering these techniques, web developers can create responsive and visually appealing web pages. Understanding when to use each method and combining them when necessary allows for creative and effective layouts. In the following sections, we'll delve into responsive web design principles and CSS preprocessors to enhance your front-end development skills.

4.4 Responsive Web Design

Responsive web design is a fundamental aspect of modern web development. With the ever-increasing variety of devices and screen sizes, creating websites that adapt to different environments is crucial. In this section, we will dive deep into responsive web design principles and provide practical examples to help you understand and implement responsive designs effectively.

Understanding Responsive Web Design

Responsive web design is an approach that allows web pages to adapt to various screen sizes and resolutions. It ensures that a website looks and functions well on everything from large desktop monitors to small mobile phones. Here are the key concepts:

1. Fluid Layouts:

To create responsive designs, use relative units like percentages rather than fixed units like pixels for layout elements. For example:

```css
.container {
  width: 90%; /* Fluid width container */
}
```

2. Media Queries:

Media queries are CSS rules that apply styles based on the characteristics of the device or viewport. They allow you to define specific CSS for different screen sizes. For example:

```css
@media (max-width: 768px) {
  /* Styles for screens smaller than 768px wide */
  .navigation {
    display: none; /* Hide navigation on small screens */
  }
}
```

3. Flexible Images:

Images should also adapt to different screen sizes. You can use CSS to set a maximum width of 100% to ensure images scale proportionally:

```css
img {
  max-width: 100%; /* Ensure images don't overflow their containers */
  height: auto; /* Maintain aspect ratio */
}
```

4. Mobile-First Approach:

Start designing for mobile screens first and then progressively enhance the design for larger screens using media queries.

Practical Examples:

1. Creating a Responsive Navigation Menu: Walk through building a navigation menu that adapts to different screen sizes, possibly collapsing into a mobile menu for smaller screens.

2. Designing a Responsive Grid Layout: Demonstrate how to create a responsive grid layout that rearranges and resizes elements on various devices.

3. Optimizing Forms for Mobile Devices: Show how to design forms that are user-friendly on both desktop and mobile screens.

Testing and Debugging:

Explain the importance of testing your responsive design on various devices and browsers. Mention tools like the browser's developer tools and online emulators.

Conclusion

Responsive web design is essential in today's multi-device world. By following the principles and examples outlined in this chapter, you'll be well-equipped to create websites that provide an optimal user experience, regardless of the device being used. In the next section, we'll explore CSS preprocessors, which can streamline your CSS workflow and make managing stylesheets more efficient.

4.5 CSS Preprocessors

CSS preprocessors are powerful tools that streamline and enhance the process of writing CSS. They introduce features and capabilities that make it easier to manage and maintain your stylesheets. In this section, we'll explore what CSS preprocessors are, how to set them up, and how to use them effectively.

Understanding CSS Preprocessors

CSS preprocessors are scripting languages that extend the capabilities of CSS. They introduce features like variables, nesting, functions, and mixins, which allow you to write cleaner and more maintainable stylesheets. The most popular CSS preprocessors are Sass (Syntactically Awesome Style Sheets) and Less.

Setting Up a CSS Preprocessor

To start using a CSS preprocessor, follow these general steps:

1. Installation: You need to install the preprocessor on your development machine. This typically involves using a package manager like npm for Node.js-based preprocessors (Sass) or downloading and installing a standalone compiler (Less).

2. Integration with Your Workflow: Integrate the preprocessor into your development workflow. For example, you can watch for changes to your preprocessor files and automatically compile them into standard CSS.

Key Features of CSS Preprocessors

Now, let's dive into some of the key features of CSS preprocessors:

1. Variables:

Variables allow you to define reusable values that can be used throughout your stylesheet. This is incredibly useful for storing things like colors, font sizes, and spacing values.

Example (Sass):

```scss
$primary-color: #3498db;
$font-size: 16px;

body {
  font-size: $font-size;
  background-color: $primary-color;
}
```

2. Nesting:

Nesting lets you write nested selectors, which makes your styles more organized and easier to read.

Example (Sass):

```scss
nav {
  ul {
    list-style: none;
  }

  li {
    display: inline;
  }
}
```

3. Mixins:

Mixins allow you to define reusable blocks of styles. You can think of them as functions for your CSS.

Example (Sass):

```scss
@mixin border-radius($radius) {
  -webkit-border-radius: $radius;
  -moz-border-radius: $radius;
  border-radius: $radius;
```

```scss
}

.button {
  @include border-radius(5px);
}
```

4. Functions:

Functions let you perform operations on values and return a result. This can be useful for calculations and dynamic styling.

Example (Sass):

```scss
$base-font-size: 16px;

body {
  font-size: $base-font-size * 1.5;
}
```

5. Importing:

You can split your styles into multiple files and import them into a single stylesheet. This promotes modularity and maintainability.

Example (Sass):

```scss
@import 'variables';

@import 'buttons';
```

Using CSS Preprocessors in Practice

Provide examples of how to set up a project to use a CSS preprocessor, including installation instructions and configuration details. Walk through the process of creating variables, mixins, and nested styles.

Conclusion

CSS preprocessors are valuable tools for improving your CSS workflow. They offer features that simplify styling, enhance code organization, and promote code reusability. By incorporating a preprocessor like Sass or Less into your development process, you'll find yourself writing more efficient and maintainable CSS. In the next section, we'll explore advanced CSS layout techniques that will help you create complex and responsive layouts with ease.

CHAPTER V
JavaScript Fundamentals

5.1 Introduction to JavaScript

JavaScript is a versatile and essential programming language for web development. It allows you to add interactivity and dynamic behavior to your websites, making them more engaging and user-friendly. In this section, we'll provide a comprehensive introduction to JavaScript, covering its history, basic syntax, and how to include it in your web pages.

What is JavaScript?

JavaScript is a high-level, interpreted scripting language primarily used for adding functionality to web pages. It was created by Brendan Eich while he was at Netscape Communications Corporation in 1995. JavaScript is not related to Java; the similar names are a historical coincidence. It is often referred to as the "language of the web" because it's supported by all major web browsers and is an integral part of front-end web development.

How to Include JavaScript in Your Web Pages

You can include JavaScript in your HTML documents in several ways:

1. Inline JavaScript: You can include JavaScript code directly within your HTML file using the `<script>` element, either within the `<head>` section or at the end of the `<body>` section.

Example (Inline JavaScript in the `<head>` section):

```html
<!DOCTYPE html>
<html>
<head>
  <title>My Web Page</title>
  <script>
    // JavaScript code goes here
    function showMessage() {
      alert("Hello, World!");
    }
  </script>
</head>
<body>
  <button onclick="showMessage()">Click me</button>
</body>
</html>
```

2. External JavaScript: It's a good practice to separate your JavaScript code into external `.js` files and then link to them using the `<script>` element's `src` attribute.

Example (External JavaScript):

```html
<!DOCTYPE html>
```

```html
<html>
<head>
  <title>My Web Page</title>
  <script src="myscript.js"></script>
</head>
<body>
  <button onclick="showMessage()">Click me</button>
</body>
</html>
```

Contents of `myscript.js`:

```javascript
// JavaScript code in myscript.js
function showMessage() {
  alert("Hello, World!");
}
```

Basic Syntax

JavaScript has a C-style syntax and is case-sensitive. Here are some key elements of JavaScript syntax:

- Statements are terminated by semicolons (`;`).

- Variables are declared using keywords like `var`, `let`, or `const`.

- Comments can be added using `//` for single-line comments or `/* */` for multi-line comments.

Example:
```javascript
// This is a single-line comment
/* This is a
multi-line comment */
```

- Functions are blocks of reusable code defined using the `function` keyword.

Example:
```javascript
function greet(name) {
    console.log("Hello, " + name + "!");
}
greet("John"); // Output: Hello, John!
```

- Data types include strings, numbers, booleans, objects, arrays, and more.

Example:
```javascript
var name = "John";
```

```javascript
var age = 30;

var isStudent = true;

var person = { firstName: "John", lastName: "Doe" };

var colors = ["red", "green", "blue"];
```

- Operators are used for performing operations on variables and values, such as addition (`+`), subtraction (`-`), equality (`==`), and logical AND (`&&`).

Example:
```javascript
var x = 5;

var y = 10;

var sum = x + y; // sum is 15
```

Conclusion

JavaScript is a powerful and essential language for web development. In this introductory section, we've covered its history, ways to include it in your web pages, basic syntax, and key concepts. Understanding these fundamentals is crucial for diving deeper into JavaScript programming, which we will explore in subsequent sections of this chapter.

Next up, in **Chapter 5: JavaScript Fundamentals, Section 2,** we will delve into "Variables, Data Types, and Operators," which are the building blocks of JavaScript programming.

5.2 Variables, Data Types, and Operators

In this section, we will delve into the fundamental building blocks of JavaScript: variables, data types, and operators. These concepts are crucial for writing dynamic and interactive web applications. We'll cover each topic in detail, provide examples, and explain the concepts step by step.

Variables

Variables in JavaScript are used to store and manipulate data. They act as containers that hold values, which can be of various data types. To declare a variable, you can use the `var`, `let`, or `const` keyword, depending on whether you want to allow reassignment or not.

```javascript
var name = "John"; // Declaring a variable using var (older way)

let age = 30;      // Declaring a variable using let (block-scoped)

const PI = 3.14;   // Declaring a constant variable using const
```

- `var`: Variables declared with `var` are function-scoped, meaning they are accessible within the function where they are defined.

- `let`: Variables declared with `let` are block-scoped, which means they are limited to the block (enclosed within curly braces) where they are defined.

- `const`: Constants declared with `const` cannot be reassigned after their initial assignment.

Data Types

JavaScript supports several data types, including:

1. Primitive Data Types:

- **String:** Used for text.

- **Number:** Used for numeric values (integers and floating-point numbers).

- **Boolean:** Represents true or false.

- **Undefined:** A variable that has been declared but not assigned a value.

- **Null:** Represents the intentional absence of any object value.

2. Composite Data Types:

- **Object:** Used for collections of key-value pairs (e.g., objects and arrays).

- **Array:** An ordered list of values.

- **Function:** A reusable block of code.

Operators

Operators in JavaScript are used for performing operations on variables and values. Here are some commonly used operators:

1. Arithmetic Operators:

- `+` (Addition)

- `-` (Subtraction)

- `*` (Multiplication)

- `/` (Division)

- `%` (Modulus)

Example:

```javascript
let a = 10;
let b = 5;
let sum = a + b; // sum will be 15
```

2. Comparison Operators:

- `==` (Equality)

- `!=` (Inequality)

- `===` (Strict Equality)

- `!==` (Strict Inequality)

- `>` (Greater Than)

- `<` (Less Than)

- `>=` (Greater Than or Equal To)

- `<=` (Less Than or Equal To)

Example:

```javascript
let x = 10;

let y = 5;

let result = x > y; // result will be true
```

3. Logical Operators:

- `&&` (Logical AND)

- `||` (Logical OR)

- `!` (Logical NOT)

Example:

```javascript
let isAdult = true;

let hasLicense = false;

let canDrive = isAdult && hasLicense; // canDrive will be false
```

4. Assignment Operators:

- `=` (Assignment)

- `+=` (Add and Assign)

- `-=` (Subtract and Assign)

- `*=` (Multiply and Assign)

- `/=` (Divide and Assign)

Example:

```javascript
let count = 5;
count += 2; // count will be 7
```

5. Concatenation Operator:

- `+` (String concatenation)

Example:

```javascript
let firstName = "John";
let lastName = "Doe";
let fullName = firstName + " " + lastName; // fullName will be "John Doe"
```

These are the foundational concepts of JavaScript variables, data types, and operators. Understanding them is essential for building more complex JavaScript applications and working with the Document Object Model (DOM), which we will explore in the next section.

Next up, in **Chapter 5: JavaScript Fundamentals, Section 3**, we will cover "Control Structures and Functions," which are crucial for controlling the flow of your JavaScript code and creating reusable code blocks.

5.3 Control Structures and Functions

In this section, we will explore control structures and functions in JavaScript. These fundamental concepts are crucial for controlling the flow of your JavaScript code and creating reusable code blocks. We will cover decision-making with conditional statements, loops for repetitive tasks, and the creation and usage of functions.

Conditional Statements

Conditional statements allow your code to make decisions and execute different actions based on certain conditions. There are three main types of conditional statements in JavaScript:

1. if Statement: The `if` statement is used for executing a block of code only if a specified condition is true.

Example:

```javascript
let age = 18;
if (age >= 18) {
    console.log("You are an adult.");
} else {
    console.log("You are not an adult.");
}
```

2. else-if Statement: The `else-if` statement is used when you have multiple conditions to check.

Example:
```javascript
let grade = 85;
if (grade >= 90) {
    console.log("A");
} else if (grade >= 80) {
    console.log("B");
} else {
    console.log("C");
}
```

3. switch Statement: The `switch` statement is used for selecting one of many code blocks to be executed.

Example:
```javascript
let day = "Monday";
switch (day) {
    case "Monday":
        console.log("It's the start of the week.");
        break;
```

```
    case "Friday":

        console.log("It's almost the weekend.");

        break;

    default:

        console.log("It's an ordinary day.");

}
```

Loops

Loops are used for executing a block of code repeatedly. JavaScript supports several types of loops:

1. for Loop: The `for` loop is used for iterating over a range of values.

Example:
```javascript
for (let i = 0; i < 5; i++) {

    console.log("Iteration " + (i + 1));

}
```

2. while Loop: The `while` loop is used when you want to execute a block of code as long as a condition is true.

Example:

```javascript
let count = 0;
while (count < 3) {
    console.log("Count: " + count);
    count++;
}
```

3. do-while Loop: The `do-while` loop is similar to the `while` loop but ensures that the code block is executed at least once, even if the condition is false.

Example:

```javascript
let num = 5;
do {
    console.log("Number: " + num);
    num--;
} while (num > 0);
```

Functions

Functions are reusable blocks of code that can be called with specific arguments to perform a task. They help organize and modularize your code. Here's how you can create and use functions in JavaScript:

```javascript
// Function declaration
function greet(name) {
    console.log("Hello, " + name + "!");
}

// Function call
greet("John"); // Output: Hello, John!
```

Functions can also return values:

```javascript
function add(a, b) {
    return a + b;
}

let result = add(3, 5); // result is 8
```

Conclusion

Control structures and functions are fundamental to JavaScript programming. They enable you to create logic that responds to different conditions and perform repetitive tasks efficiently. Mastering these concepts is essential for building dynamic and interactive web applications.

Next, in **Chapter 5: JavaScript Fundamentals, Section 4,** we will dive into "Working with the Document Object Model (DOM)," which is crucial for manipulating web page content and creating interactive web experiences.

5.4 Working with the Document Object Model (DOM)

In this section, we will delve into the Document Object Model (DOM), which is a critical aspect of JavaScript for creating dynamic and interactive web pages. The DOM represents the structure of an HTML document and allows you to manipulate its content and structure using JavaScript.

What is the Document Object Model (DOM)?

The Document Object Model (DOM) is a programming interface for web documents. It represents the page so that programs can change the document structure, style, and content dynamically. Essentially, the DOM is a tree-like representation of the HTML elements on a web page, where each element is represented as an object with properties and methods that can be manipulated using JavaScript.

Accessing DOM Elements

To work with the DOM, you need to access elements within the HTML document. There are several methods for selecting DOM elements:

1. getElementById: Selects an element by its `id` attribute.

```javascript
let element = document.getElementById("myElement");
```

2. getElementsByClassName: Selects elements by their `class` attribute.

```javascript
let elements = document.getElementsByClassName("myClass");
```

3. getElementsByTagName: Selects elements by their tag name (e.g., `div`, `p`, `h1`).

```javascript
let elements = document.getElementsByTagName("p");
```

4. querySelector: Selects the first element that matches a CSS selector.

```javascript
let element = document.querySelector("#myElement");
```

5. querySelectorAll: Selects all elements that match a CSS selector.

```javascript
let elements = document.querySelectorAll(".myClass");
```

Modifying DOM Elements

Once you've selected a DOM element, you can manipulate it in various ways:

1. Changing Text and HTML Content: You can modify the text or HTML content of an element.

```javascript
let element = document.getElementById("myElement");

element.textContent = "New text content";

element.innerHTML = "<p>New HTML content</p>";
```

2. Modifying Attributes: You can change or add attributes to elements.

```javascript
let link = document.querySelector("a");

link.setAttribute("href", "https://example.com");
```

3. Styling Elements: You can apply CSS styles to elements.

```javascript
let element = document.getElementById("myElement");
```

```javascript
element.style.color = "blue";

element.style.backgroundColor = "yellow";
```

Creating and Appending Elements

You can create new DOM elements and append them to the document:

```javascript
// Create a new element
let newElement = document.createElement("div");

// Set its attributes and content
newElement.className = "new-class";

newElement.textContent = "New element content";

// Append it to an existing element
let container = document.getElementById("container");

container.appendChild(newElement);
```

Event Handling

The DOM allows you to add event listeners to elements, enabling you to respond to user interactions such as clicks, keypresses, and mouse movements.

```javascript
let button = document.getElementById("myButton");

button.addEventListener("click", function () {
    alert("Button clicked!");
});
```

Conclusion

Working with the Document Object Model (DOM) is essential for creating dynamic and interactive web pages. You can access, manipulate, and modify HTML elements, attributes, and styles using JavaScript. Understanding how to interact with the DOM is a fundamental skill for front-end web development.

Next, in **Chapter 5: JavaScript Fundamentals, Section 5,** we will cover "Debugging JavaScript," which is crucial for identifying and fixing errors in your code to ensure your web applications run smoothly.

5.5 Debugging JavaScript

Debugging is a critical skill for any programmer, including JavaScript developers. It involves identifying and fixing errors or bugs in your code to ensure your web applications run smoothly. In this section, we will explore various debugging techniques and tools available for JavaScript.

Types of JavaScript Errors

JavaScript errors can be categorized into several common types:

1. Syntax Errors: These occur when your code violates the rules of the JavaScript language. They are usually detected by the browser's JavaScript engine during code execution.

Example:

```javascript
let x = 10;
console.log(x;
// SyntaxError: Unexpected token ';'
```

2. Runtime Errors: These occur during code execution when something unexpected happens. Common runtime errors include referencing undefined variables or dividing by zero.

Example:

```javascript
```

```javascript
let y = 5;

let z = y / 0;

// Uncaught TypeError: Cannot divide by zero
```

3. Logical Errors: These are the most challenging to detect and fix because they do not produce error messages. Instead, they result in unintended behavior or incorrect output.

Example:

```javascript
function calculateTotal(price, quantity) {

   return price * quantity;

}

let total = calculateTotal(10, 2);

console.log(total); // Outputs 100 instead of 20
```

Debugging Techniques

1. Console Logging: Use `console.log()` to print variables and messages to the browser's console. This is a simple and effective way to inspect values and the flow of your code.

```javascript
```

```javascript
let name = "John";

console.log("Hello, " + name);
```

2. Breakpoints: Most modern browsers come with developer tools that allow you to set breakpoints in your code. When execution reaches a breakpoint, it pauses, and you can inspect variables and the call stack.

Example:

```javascript
function greet(name) {

    debugger; // Set a breakpoint here

    console.log("Hello, " + name);

}

greet("John");
```

3. Try-Catch Blocks: Use `try...catch` blocks to handle exceptions gracefully and log detailed error messages.

Example:

```javascript
try {

    let result = 10 / 0;

} catch (error) {
```

```
    console.error("An error occurred: " + error.message);
  }
  ```
```

**Browser Developer Tools**

Browser developer tools provide a rich set of debugging features. To access them:

**1. Google Chrome:** Press `F12` or right-click on the page and select "Inspect." Go to the "Console" tab for logging and debugging.

**2. Mozilla Firefox:** Press `F12` or right-click on the page and select "Inspect Element." Go to the "Console" tab.

**3. Microsoft Edge:** Press `F12` or right-click and select "Inspect." Go to the "Console" tab.

These tools allow you to set breakpoints, inspect variables, step through code, and monitor network activity.

**Debugging Tips**

Here are some additional tips for effective debugging:

- Start by reading error messages carefully. They often provide valuable information about the issue.
```

- Divide your code into smaller functions and test each one separately.

- Use descriptive variable and function names to make your code more readable.

- Comment out sections of code to isolate the problem.

- Utilize the browser's developer tools to their fullest extent.

Conclusion

Debugging JavaScript is an essential skill for web developers. By understanding the types of errors, employing debugging techniques, and using browser developer tools effectively, you can diagnose and resolve issues in your code efficiently. Debugging is a crucial part of the development process that ensures your JavaScript applications work as intended.

This concludes our exploration of JavaScript fundamentals in Chapter 5. With a solid understanding of these concepts, you are well-equipped to start building dynamic and interactive web applications using JavaScript.

CHAPTER VI
Modern JavaScript and ES6

6.1 Introduction to ES6

ES6, also known as ECMAScript 2015, brought significant enhancements to the JavaScript language, making it more powerful and expressive. In this section, we will introduce you to ES6 and its key features, including let and const, arrow functions, and template literals.

What is ES6?

ES6 stands for ECMAScript 2015, which is a standardized version of JavaScript introduced to provide developers with new features and syntax improvements. ES6 is widely supported in modern browsers, making it essential for modern web development. Let's explore some of its key features:

Block-Scoped Declarations with `let` and `const`

In ES6, the `let` and `const` keywords were introduced to declare variables with block-level scope, unlike `var`, which has function-level scope.

- `let`: Declares a mutable (modifiable) variable that can be reassigned.

Example:

```javascript
```

```javascript
let message = "Hello";
message = "Hi"; // Valid
```

- `const`: Declares a variable as a constant, which cannot be reassigned after the initial assignment.

Example:
```javascript
const pi = 3.14;
pi = 3.14159; // Invalid
```

Arrow Functions

Arrow functions provide a concise syntax for writing functions in ES6. They are especially useful for anonymous functions and functions with a single expression.

Example:
```javascript
// ES5 function expression
let add = function (a, b) {
    return a + b;
};
```

```
// ES6 arrow function

let add = (a, b) => a + b;
```

Template Literals

Template literals allow you to create multi-line strings and embed expressions within them using `${}`. This makes string interpolation and formatting much more convenient.

Example:

```javascript
let name = "John";

let greeting = `Hello, ${name}!

How are you today?`;

console.log(greeting);
```

Default Parameters

ES6 introduced default parameter values for functions, which simplify function definitions and provide fallback values if arguments are not provided.

Example:

```javascript
function greet(name = "Guest") {
```

```javascript
  console.log(`Hello, ${name}!`);
}
greet(); // Outputs: Hello, Guest!
greet("John"); // Outputs: Hello, John!
```

Object Destructuring

Destructuring allows you to extract values from objects and assign them to variables with the same names as the object's properties.

Example:
```javascript
let person = { firstName: "John", lastName: "Doe" };
let { firstName, lastName } = person;
console.log(firstName); // Outputs: John
```

Spread and Rest Operators

The spread (`...`) and rest (`...`) operators allow you to work with arrays and function arguments more efficiently.

- Spread operator: Expands an array into individual elements.

Example:

```javascript
let numbers = [1, 2, 3];

let allNumbers = [...numbers, 4, 5];

console.log(allNumbers); // Outputs: [1, 2, 3, 4, 5]
```

- Rest operator: Collects remaining arguments into an array.

Example:

```javascript
function sum(...numbers) {

    return numbers.reduce((total, num) => total + num, 0);

}

console.log(sum(1, 2, 3, 4, 5)); // Outputs: 15
```

Conclusion

ES6 introduced many valuable features that enhance the JavaScript language, making it more powerful and expressive. In this section, we've covered block-scoped declarations with `let` and `const`, arrow functions, template literals, default parameters, object destructuring, and the spread/rest operators. Understanding these features is crucial for modern JavaScript development.

Next, in **Chapter 6: Modern JavaScript and ES6, Section 2,** we will delve deeper into "Arrow Functions and Template Literals," providing more detailed examples and explanations for these ES6 features.

6.2 Arrow Functions and Template Literals

In this section, we'll dive into two significant features introduced in ES6: Arrow Functions and Template Literals. These features provide concise and expressive ways to work with functions and strings in JavaScript.

Arrow Functions

Arrow functions, also known as fat arrow functions, offer a more compact syntax for writing functions. They are especially useful for functions with simple expressions. Let's explore the syntax and benefits of arrow functions.

Syntax of Arrow Functions

The basic syntax of an arrow function is as follows:

```javascript
const functionName = (parameters) => expression;
```

- `functionName`: The name of the function (optional).

- `parameters`: The list of input parameters (optional).

- `expression`: The expression to be evaluated and returned.

Examples of Arrow Functions

1. A basic arrow function without parameters:

```javascript
const sayHello = () => {
   console.log("Hello, world!");
};


sayHello(); // Outputs: Hello, world!
```

2. Arrow function with parameters:

```javascript
const add = (a, b) => {
   return a + b;
};


console.log(add(5, 3)); // Outputs: 8
```

3. Arrow function with implicit return:

```javascript
const multiply = (a, b) => a * b;


console.log(multiply(4, 2)); // Outputs: 8
```

4. Arrow functions in arrays:

```javascript
const numbers = [1, 2, 3, 4];


const squaredNumbers = numbers.map((num) => num  2);


console.log(squaredNumbers); // Outputs: [1, 4, 9, 16]
```

Template Literals

Template literals provide a more flexible and readable way to work with strings in JavaScript. They allow you to embed expressions and create multi-line strings. Here's how template literals work.

Syntax of Template Literals

Template literals are enclosed in backticks (`` ` ``) instead of single or double quotes. To embed expressions within template literals, you use `` `${expression}` ``.

Examples of Template Literals

1. Basic usage of template literals:

```javascript
const name = "John";
const greeting = `Hello, ${name}!`;

console.log(greeting); // Outputs: Hello, John!
```

2. Multi-line strings using template literals:

```javascript
const message = `
    This is a
    multi-line
    string.`;

console.log(message);
/* Outputs:
```

   This is a

   multi-line

   string.

*/

```

3. Evaluating expressions within template literals:

```javascript
const x = 5;
const y = 3;
const result = `The sum of ${x} and ${y} is ${x + y}.`;


console.log(result); // Outputs: The sum of 5 and 3 is 8.
```

Benefits and Use Cases

- Arrow functions provide a more concise and readable way to define functions, especially for short functions like event handlers and callbacks.

- Template literals make string interpolation and multi-line string creation much more straightforward, improving the readability of your code.
```

Conclusion

Arrow functions and template literals are essential features introduced in ES6 that enhance the JavaScript language's expressiveness and readability. Arrow functions simplify function definitions, while template literals offer a more flexible way to work with strings. Understanding and using these features is crucial for modern JavaScript development.

In the next section, **Destructuring and Spread/Rest Operators**, we will explore how destructuring and spread/rest operators in ES6 can simplify data manipulation and function arguments.

6.3 Destructuring and Spread/Rest Operators

In this section, we'll explore two powerful features introduced in ES6: Destructuring and Spread/Rest Operators. These features simplify data manipulation and function arguments, making your code more concise and readable.

Destructuring

Destructuring allows you to extract values from objects and arrays and assign them to variables. This feature is particularly useful when working with complex data structures.

Destructuring Objects

Let's start with object destructuring:

```javascript
const person = {
   firstName: "John",
   lastName: "Doe",
   age: 30,
};

// Destructuring object properties
const { firstName, lastName, age } = person;
```

```javascript
console.log(firstName); // Outputs: John
```

You can also rename variables during destructuring:

```javascript
const { firstName: fName, lastName: lName } = person;

console.log(fName); // Outputs: John
```

Destructuring Arrays

Destructuring arrays is similarly straightforward:

```javascript
const colors = ["red", "green", "blue"];

// Destructuring array elements
const [firstColor, secondColor, thirdColor] = colors;

console.log(firstColor); // Outputs: red
```

```
```
```

Destructuring can be especially useful when working with functions that return objects or arrays:

```javascript
function getPerson() {
    return {
        firstName: "John",
        lastName: "Doe",
    };
}


const { firstName, lastName } = getPerson();
```

Spread Operator

The spread operator (`...`) allows you to expand arrays and objects into their individual elements. It's commonly used for creating new arrays or objects based on existing ones.

Spread Operator with Arrays

Here's how you can use the spread operator with arrays:
```

```javascript
const numbers = [1, 2, 3];
const moreNumbers = [...numbers, 4, 5];


console.log(moreNumbers); // Outputs: [1, 2, 3, 4, 5]
```

Spread Operator with Objects

With objects, the spread operator can be used to merge or clone objects:

```javascript
const person = { firstName: "John" };
const details = { lastName: "Doe", age: 30 };


const mergedPerson = { ...person, ...details };


console.log(mergedPerson);
// Outputs: { firstName: "John", lastName: "Doe", age: 30 }
```

Rest Operator

The rest operator (`...`) allows you to collect the remaining elements into an array. It's often used in function parameters to accept a variable number of arguments.

```javascript
function sum(...numbers) {
    return numbers.reduce((total, num) => total + num, 0);
}


console.log(sum(1, 2, 3, 4, 5)); // Outputs: 15
```

Benefits and Use Cases

- Destructuring simplifies the extraction of values from objects and arrays, making your code more concise.

- The spread operator is useful for creating new arrays and objects based on existing ones, merging objects, and expanding arrays.

- The rest operator simplifies working with variable numbers of function arguments.

Conclusion

Destructuring and the spread/rest operators introduced in ES6 are powerful tools that enhance the readability and expressiveness of your JavaScript code. Understanding how to use them to manipulate data structures and function arguments is crucial for modern JavaScript development.

In the next section, **Promises and Async/Await,** we will explore asynchronous programming in JavaScript using promises and the `async/await` syntax, which simplifies working with asynchronous code.

6.4 Promises and Async/Await

In this section, we will delve into asynchronous programming in JavaScript, specifically focusing on Promises and the `async/await` syntax. These features were introduced in ES6 and have become essential for managing asynchronous operations in a more readable and organized way.

Introduction to Promises

Promises are a way to handle asynchronous operations in a more structured manner. They represent a value that might be available now, in the future, or never. A Promise can be in one of three states:

- Pending: The initial state, representing a task that is still executing.

- Fulfilled: The task completed successfully, and a result is available.

- Rejected: The task encountered an error or was unsuccessful.

Creating a Promise

You can create a Promise using the `Promise` constructor. It takes a function with two arguments: `resolve` and `reject`.

```javascript
const myPromise = new Promise((resolve, reject) => {
    // Asynchronous operation
    setTimeout(() => {
```

```javascript
    const success = true;

    if (success) {

      resolve("Promise resolved!");

    } else {

      reject("Promise rejected!");

    }

  }, 1000);

});
```

Consuming a Promise

To use the result of a Promise, you can use the `.then()` and `.catch()` methods. The `.then()` method is called when the Promise is fulfilled, and the `.catch()` method handles rejection.

```javascript
myPromise

  .then((result) => {

    console.log(result); // Outputs: Promise resolved!

  })

  .catch((error) => {

    console.error(error);

  });
```

Async/Await

The `async/await` syntax simplifies asynchronous code even further. It allows you to write asynchronous code that looks similar to synchronous code, making it more readable and maintainable.

Using `async` Functions

To define an `async` function, you prepend the `async` keyword to the function declaration. Inside an `async` function, you can use the `await` keyword to pause execution until a Promise is settled.

```javascript
async function fetchData() {
    try {
        const response = await fetch("https://api.example.com/data");
        const data = await response.json();
        return data;
    } catch (error) {
        throw new Error("Failed to fetch data");
    }
}
```

Using `await` in Promises

In non-`async` functions or blocks, you can still use the `await` keyword within a Promise chain to pause execution until the Promise is fulfilled.

```javascript
function fetchData() {

  fetch("https://api.example.com/data")

    .then((response) => response.json())

    .then((data) => {

      // Process data

    })

    .catch((error) => {

      console.error(error);

    });

}
```

Benefits and Use Cases

- Promises and `async/await` simplify asynchronous code, making it easier to read and maintain.

- Promises are particularly useful when dealing with multiple asynchronous tasks, such as making API requests.

- `async/await` is beneficial when you want to write asynchronous code that closely resembles synchronous code.

Conclusion

Promises and the `async/await` syntax are essential tools for handling asynchronous operations in JavaScript. They provide a structured and readable way to work with asynchronous code, making your programs more maintainable and error-resistant.

In the next section, **Modules and Classes**, we will explore how ES6 introduced modules for organizing code and how classes offer a more structured approach to object-oriented programming in JavaScript.

6.5 Modules and Classes

In this section, we will explore two essential features introduced in ES6: Modules and Classes. These features enhance the structure and organization of JavaScript code, making it more modular and object-oriented.

Modules

ES6 introduced native support for modules in JavaScript, allowing you to split your code into smaller, reusable pieces. Modules help you manage dependencies, improve code organization, and make it easier to collaborate on projects.

Creating a Module

To create a module, you can use the `export` keyword to specify what should be accessible from the module.

```javascript
// myModule.js
export const add = (a, b) => a + b;
export const subtract = (a, b) => a - b;
```

Importing a Module

You can import functions, variables, or classes from a module using the `import` statement.

```javascript
import { add, subtract } from "./myModule.js";

console.log(add(5, 3)); // Outputs: 8
console.log(subtract(5, 3)); // Outputs: 2
```

Default Exports

You can also have a default export in a module, allowing you to export a single "main" thing from the module.

```javascript
// myModule.js
const greeting = "Hello, world!";
export default greeting;
```

```javascript
// Importing the default export
import greeting from "./myModule.js";
```

```javascript
console.log(greeting); // Outputs: Hello, world!
```

Classes

Classes in ES6 provide a more structured way to create objects and work with object-oriented programming principles like inheritance and encapsulation.

Defining a Class

To define a class, use the `class` keyword, followed by the class name.

```javascript
class Person {
  constructor(firstName, lastName) {
    this.firstName = firstName;
    this.lastName = lastName;
  }

  getFullName() {
    return `${this.firstName} ${this.lastName}`;
  }
}
```

Creating Objects

You can create objects from a class using the `new` keyword.

```javascript
const john = new Person("John", "Doe");
console.log(john.getFullName()); // Outputs: John Doe
```

Inheritance

ES6 classes support inheritance through the `extends` keyword, allowing you to create subclasses that inherit properties and methods from a parent class.

```javascript
class Student extends Person {
  constructor(firstName, lastName, studentId) {
    super(firstName, lastName);
    this.studentId = studentId;
  }
}
```

Static Methods

Static methods are defined on the class itself, rather than on instances of the class. They are useful for utility functions related to the class.

```javascript
class MathUtils {
  static add(a, b) {
    return a + b;
  }
}

console.log(MathUtils.add(5, 3)); // Outputs: 8
```

Benefits and Use Cases

- Modules help organize and modularize code, making it easier to manage large codebases.

- Classes provide a more structured and object-oriented approach to creating and working with objects.

- Combining modules and classes allows you to build well-structured and maintainable applications.

Conclusion

Modules and classes introduced in ES6 have revolutionized JavaScript development. Modules enable better code organization and dependency management, while classes provide a more structured way to create and work with objects. Understanding and utilizing these features are essential for modern JavaScript development.

This concludes our exploration of Chapter 6: Modern JavaScript and ES6. With a solid grasp of the concepts covered in this chapter, you are well-prepared to develop modern and maintainable JavaScript applications.

CHAPTER VII
Web Performance Optimization

7.1 Understanding Website Performance

In this section, we will explore the critical aspects of website performance, including why it matters, what factors affect it, and how to measure and improve it.

Why Website Performance Matters

Website performance plays a crucial role in user experience and can have a significant impact on various aspects of your online presence, including:

1. User Engagement: Faster-loading websites tend to have higher user engagement and lower bounce rates. Users are more likely to stay and interact with your content.

2. Search Engine Ranking: Search engines, such as Google, consider page speed as a ranking factor. Faster websites are more likely to appear higher in search results.

3. Conversion Rates: Improved performance can lead to higher conversion rates, which is vital for e-commerce websites and online businesses.

4. Mobile Friendliness: Fast-loading websites are essential for mobile users who may have limited bandwidth and slower devices.

Factors Affecting Website Performance

Several factors can impact website performance:

1. Page Size: The size of web pages, including images, scripts, and stylesheets, affects load times. Large files take longer to download.

2. Server Response Time: The time it takes for your server to respond to a request can impact performance. A slow server can lead to slow page rendering.

3. Render Blocking: JavaScript and CSS that block the rendering of a page can delay the display of content.

4. Image Optimization: Large, uncompressed images can significantly increase page load times. Optimizing images is crucial for performance.

5. Caching: Proper caching strategies can reduce server load and improve load times for returning visitors.

Measuring Website Performance

To understand and improve website performance, you need to measure it. Several tools and metrics can help you assess your website's performance:

1. Page Speed Insights: A tool from Google that analyzes your website's performance and provides recommendations for improvement.

2. Lighthouse: An open-source tool for auditing and improving web page quality. It provides performance, accessibility, and SEO audits.

3. WebPageTest: A free tool that allows you to test the performance of your website from multiple locations and devices.

4. Chrome DevTools: Built into the Google Chrome browser, it provides performance profiling, network analysis, and various performance-related metrics.

Improving Website Performance

Here are some key strategies for improving website performance:

1. Optimize Images: Use compressed and appropriately sized images. Consider using modern image formats like WebP.

2. Minimize HTTP Requests: Reduce the number of requests by combining CSS and JavaScript files and using CSS sprites for icons.

3. Leverage Browser Caching: Set caching headers to allow browsers to cache static assets and reduce server load.

4. Enable Compression: Use GZIP or Brotli compression to reduce the size of text-based assets like HTML, CSS, and JavaScript.

5. Eliminate Render-Blocking Resources: Move JavaScript to the bottom of the page or use the `async` or `defer` attributes to load scripts asynchronously.

6. Content Delivery Network (CDN): Use a CDN to distribute your content globally and reduce latency for users.

Conclusion

Understanding website performance is essential for delivering a fast and responsive user experience. Slow-loading websites can lead to high bounce rates, lower search engine rankings, and decreased user satisfaction. By measuring and optimizing performance factors like page size, server response time, and render-blocking resources, you can significantly improve the speed and overall performance of your website. In the next sections, we will dive deeper into specific techniques and tools for optimizing web performance.

7.2 Techniques for Faster Loading

In this section, we'll explore various techniques to speed up the loading time of your web pages. Faster loading times improve user experience, increase engagement, and boost your website's performance.

1. Image Optimization

Images often account for a significant portion of a web page's file size. Optimizing images is crucial for faster loading.

Techniques:

- **Compression:** Use tools like ImageMagick or online services to compress images without a significant loss in quality.

- **Responsive Images:** Implement responsive images using the `srcset` attribute to serve different image sizes based on the user's device and screen size.

- **Lazy Loading:** Use the `loading="lazy"` attribute to load images only when they come into the viewport.

2. Minify CSS and JavaScript

Reducing the size of your CSS and JavaScript files can significantly improve page load times.

Techniques:

- **Minification:** Minify your CSS and JavaScript files to remove unnecessary whitespace, comments, and redundant code.

- **Concatenation:** Combine multiple CSS or JavaScript files into one to reduce the number of HTTP requests.

- **Use a CDN:** Host popular libraries like jQuery on a content delivery network (CDN) to leverage browser caching and faster loading.

3. Asynchronous Loading

Loading resources asynchronously prevents them from blocking the rendering of your page.

Techniques:

- **Async and Defer Attributes:** Use the `async` or `defer` attribute in your `<script>` tags to control when scripts are executed.

- **Preloading:** Use the `preload` attribute to inform the browser to fetch critical assets early in the page load process.

4. Browser Caching

Leveraging browser caching allows returning visitors to load your site faster.

Techniques:

- Cache-Control Headers: Set appropriate cache-control headers on your server to specify how long browsers should cache resources.

- Versioning: Append a version number or a unique identifier to the filenames of your static assets when you release updates to ensure browsers fetch the latest version.

5. Content Delivery Networks (CDNs)

CDNs distribute your website's assets across multiple servers worldwide, reducing latency and speeding up content delivery.

Techniques:

- CDN Integration: Use a CDN service to host your static files, such as images, stylesheets, and scripts.

- Edge Caching: Configure edge caching on your CDN to cache content closer to users, reducing server load and response times.

6. Critical Rendering Path Optimization

Optimize the critical rendering path to ensure that the most important content loads quickly.

Techniques:

- **Inline Critical CSS:** Inline critical CSS directly into the HTML to render above-the-fold content quickly.

- **Load JavaScript Conditionally:** Load non-essential JavaScript files after initial page rendering.

- **Server-Side Rendering (SSR):** Implement SSR for JavaScript-heavy applications to serve pre-rendered HTML.

7. HTTP/2 and HTTPS

Upgrade to HTTP/2, which is more efficient in handling multiple requests and responses, and ensure your site uses HTTPS for secure and faster connections.

Techniques:

- **Enable HTTP/2:** Check with your hosting provider or server configuration to enable HTTP/2.

- **SSL Certificates:** Obtain and configure SSL certificates to enable HTTPS.

8. Mobile Optimization

Optimize your site for mobile users to ensure fast loading times on mobile devices.

Techniques:

- **Responsive Design:** Implement responsive design principles to ensure your site adapts to various screen sizes.

- **AMP (Accelerated Mobile Pages):** Consider using AMP to create mobile-friendly, fast-loading pages.

Conclusion

Improving website loading times is essential for providing an excellent user experience and achieving better search engine rankings. By implementing techniques like image optimization, minification, asynchronous loading, caching, and leveraging CDNs, you can significantly enhance your website's performance. Always measure your site's performance with tools like PageSpeed Insights or Lighthouse and continually optimize for even faster loading times. In the next sections, we will delve into more specific aspects of web performance optimization.

7.3 Reducing Render Times

In this section, we will explore techniques for reducing render times, which is crucial for providing a snappy and responsive user experience. Render times refer to the time it takes for a web page to load and display content in the user's browser.

1. Minimize Critical Rendering Path

The critical rendering path is the sequence of steps the browser takes to render a web page. Minimizing this path speeds up the rendering process.

Techniques:

- **Optimize Critical CSS:** Identify and inline the critical CSS necessary to render above-the-fold content quickly. This prevents render-blocking stylesheets.

- **Async JavaScript:** Load non-essential JavaScript asynchronously to prevent it from blocking rendering. Use the `async` attribute or load scripts at the end of the body.

2. Efficiently Load Images

Images can significantly impact render times. Optimizing how images load is essential.

Techniques:

- **Lazy Loading:** Use the `loading="lazy"` attribute on `<img>` elements to load images only when they come into the viewport. This reduces the initial page load time.

- **Responsive Images:** Serve different image sizes based on the user's device and screen size using the `srcset` attribute.

- **Image Formats:** Use modern image formats like WebP, which typically offer better compression and smaller file sizes compared to JPEG or PNG.

3. Prioritize Visible Content

Ensure that the most critical content is prioritized and rendered first.

Techniques:

- **Critical Fonts:** Preload and prioritize loading critical fonts to avoid text reflow.

- **Inline Critical Resources:** Inline critical CSS and JavaScript to avoid additional HTTP requests.

- **Server-Side Rendering (SSR):** Implement SSR for JavaScript-heavy applications to serve pre-rendered HTML for faster initial rendering.

4. Optimize JavaScript Execution

JavaScript can significantly affect render times, especially when it blocks rendering.

Techniques:

- Code Splitting: Split large JavaScript bundles into smaller, more manageable chunks. Load only the necessary JavaScript for the current page or view.

- Async and Defer: Use the `async` or `defer` attributes on `<script>` tags to control when JavaScript is executed without blocking rendering.

- Intersection Observer: Use the Intersection Observer API to trigger JavaScript functionality when elements enter the viewport, reducing the need for costly event listeners.

5. Minimize DOM Manipulation

Frequent DOM manipulation can lead to reflows and repaints, slowing down rendering.

Techniques:

- Batch DOM Updates: When making multiple DOM changes, batch them together to minimize reflows and repaints.

- Use CSS Transitions: Animate elements using CSS transitions instead of JavaScript to leverage hardware acceleration.

- Virtual DOM: In JavaScript frameworks like React, use a virtual DOM to minimize direct DOM manipulation.

6. Monitor and Optimize with Browser DevTools

Browser DevTools provide powerful tools for monitoring and optimizing rendering performance.

Techniques:

- Performance Profiling: Use tools like Chrome DevTools' Performance panel to identify rendering bottlenecks and optimize your web page.

- Lighthouse Audits: Run Lighthouse audits to get recommendations on improving rendering performance and overall page speed.

Conclusion

Reducing render times is essential for delivering a fast and responsive user experience. By minimizing the critical rendering path, efficiently loading images, prioritizing visible content, optimizing JavaScript execution, minimizing DOM manipulation, and utilizing browser DevTools for performance profiling, you can significantly improve the rendering speed of your web pages. Continuously monitor and optimize your site's rendering performance to ensure a smooth user experience. In the following sections, we will explore lazy loading and code splitting techniques and delve deeper into browser DevTools for performance profiling.

7.4 Lazy Loading and Code Splitting

In this section, we will explore two advanced techniques, Lazy Loading and Code Splitting, that can significantly improve web page performance by optimizing the loading of assets and JavaScript code.

1. Lazy Loading Images

Lazy loading images is a technique that defers the loading of non-visible images until they are needed. This reduces the initial page load time and improves perceived performance.

How to Implement Lazy Loading for Images:

1. HTML Attribute: Add the `loading="lazy"` attribute to your `<img>` elements.

```html
<img src="image.jpg" alt="Lazy-loaded image" loading="lazy">
```

2. JavaScript: You can also implement lazy loading programmatically using JavaScript by monitoring the viewport and loading images when they come into view.

```javascript
const lazyImages = document.querySelectorAll('img[data-src]');

const lazyLoad = () => {
```

```javascript
lazyImages.forEach((img) => {
    if (img.getBoundingClientRect().top < window.innerHeight) {
        img.src = img.getAttribute('data-src');
        img.removeAttribute('data-src');
    }
  });
};


window.addEventListener('scroll', lazyLoad);
```

2. Code Splitting

Code splitting is a technique that involves breaking down your JavaScript code into smaller chunks (bundles) and loading them only when they are needed. This can significantly reduce the initial page load time.

How to Implement Code Splitting:

1. Webpack or Other Bundlers: If you're using Webpack or similar bundling tools, they often have built-in support for code splitting.

Here's an example of code splitting with Webpack:

```javascript
// webpack.config.js
```

```javascript
module.exports = {
  // ...
  optimization: {
    splitChunks: {
      chunks: 'all',
    },
  },
};
```

2. Dynamic Imports: In modern JavaScript, you can use dynamic `import()` statements to load modules on-demand.

```javascript
// Dynamically import a module
import('./moduleToLoad.js')
  .then((module) => {
    // Use the module
  })
  .catch((error) => {
    console.error('Error loading module:', error);
  });
```

3. React and Other Frameworks: If you're using a JavaScript framework like React, you can use features like React's `React.lazy()` to load components lazily.

```javascript
const LazyComponent = React.lazy(() => import('./LazyComponent'));
```

Benefits of Lazy Loading and Code Splitting

- **Faster Initial Load:** Lazy loading and code splitting reduce the initial payload, resulting in faster page load times.

- **Improved User Experience:** Users see content more quickly, leading to a better perceived performance and user experience.

- **Lower Data Usage:** Reduced data usage for users on metered connections or mobile devices.

- **Optimized SEO:** Search engines can better crawl and index your site because of faster loading times.

Conclusion

Lazy loading images and code splitting are powerful techniques for optimizing web page performance. By deferring the loading of non-essential images and JavaScript code until they are needed, you can significantly improve load times, reduce data usage, and enhance the user experience. These techniques are especially valuable for modern web applications and large websites. In the final section, we will explore how to leverage browser DevTools for performance profiling and optimization.

7.5 Browser DevTools for Performance Profiling

In this section, we will delve into the powerful tools available in browser DevTools for performance profiling and optimization. These tools enable you to diagnose performance issues, identify bottlenecks, and optimize your web pages for faster loading and rendering.

1. Chrome DevTools

Chrome DevTools is a suite of web development tools built into the Google Chrome browser. It offers several performance profiling tools to help you understand and optimize your web page's performance.

Performance Panel

The Performance panel in Chrome DevTools allows you to record and analyze page performance.

Steps:

1. Open Chrome DevTools by right-clicking on your web page and selecting "Inspect" or pressing `Ctrl+Shift+I` (or `Cmd+Option+I` on Mac).

2. Go to the "Performance" tab.

3. Click the record button (a circle) to start recording a performance profile.

4. Interact with your web page to capture performance data.

5. Click the stop button (a square) to stop recording.

Key Metrics

- **Frames Per Second (FPS):** Monitor FPS to ensure smooth animations and interactions. A low FPS indicates performance issues.

- **CPU Usage:** Identify high CPU usage during page load or interactions.

- **Network Requests:** Analyze the number and duration of network requests to optimize asset loading.

- **Memory Usage:** Monitor memory consumption to prevent memory leaks.

Flame Chart

The Flame Chart visualizes the execution timeline of your web page. It helps identify CPU-bound tasks and JavaScript execution bottlenecks.

Waterfall Chart

The Waterfall Chart provides a detailed view of network requests, including DNS resolution, connection setup, and asset loading times. Use it to diagnose slow-loading resources.

2. Lighthouse Audits

Lighthouse is an open-source tool integrated into Chrome DevTools that performs automated audits of web pages and provides recommendations for improving performance, accessibility, and SEO.

Steps:

1. Open Chrome DevTools.

2. Go to the "Lighthouse" tab.

3. Select the performance category and click "Generate report."

Lighthouse generates a report that includes performance scores and detailed suggestions for improvements.

3. Firefox Developer Tools

Firefox Developer Tools offers similar performance profiling tools to Chrome DevTools.

Performance Panel

The Performance panel in Firefox Developer Tools allows you to record and analyze performance data.

Steps:

1. Open Firefox Developer Tools by right-clicking on your web page and selecting "Inspect Element" or pressing `Ctrl+Shift+I` (or `Cmd+Option+I` on Mac).

2. Go to the "Performance" tab.

3. Click the record button to start recording a performance profile.

4. Interact with your web page to capture performance data.

5. Click the stop button to stop recording.

Network Monitor

The Network Monitor provides detailed information about network requests, including request and response headers, timings, and content sizes.

4. Microsoft Edge DevTools

Microsoft Edge DevTools offers performance profiling tools similar to those in Chrome and Firefox.

Performance Panel

The Performance panel in Microsoft Edge DevTools allows you to record and analyze performance data.

Steps:

1. Open Microsoft Edge DevTools by right-clicking on your web page and selecting "Inspect" or pressing `Ctrl+Shift+I`.

2. Go to the "Performance" tab.

3. Click the record button to start recording a performance profile.

4. Interact with your web page to capture performance data.

5. Click the stop button to stop recording.

Network Panel

The Network panel provides information about network requests, including timings, sizes, and request/response details.

Conclusion

Browser DevTools are invaluable for performance profiling and optimization. Whether you're using Chrome DevTools, Firefox Developer Tools, or Microsoft Edge DevTools, these tools provide insights into your web page's performance, including metrics, CPU usage, network requests, and more. By using these tools, you can diagnose performance issues, identify bottlenecks, and implement optimizations to deliver a fast and responsive user experience. Continuously monitor and optimize your web pages to ensure top-notch performance for your users.

CHAPTER VIII
Front-End Frameworks and Libraries

8.1 Introduction to Front-End Frameworks

In this section, we will introduce front-end frameworks and discuss their significance in modern web development. Front-end frameworks are essential tools that simplify and streamline the process of building interactive and responsive web applications.

What Are Front-End Frameworks?

Front-end frameworks are collections of pre-written, reusable code, including HTML, CSS, and JavaScript, designed to help developers create consistent, efficient, and feature-rich web applications. These frameworks provide a structure and a set of best practices for building user interfaces, which is especially crucial in today's complex web applications.

Why Use Front-End Frameworks?

Front-end frameworks offer several advantages:

1. Efficiency: They speed up development by providing pre-built components, templates, and libraries, reducing the need for writing code from scratch.

2. Consistency: Frameworks enforce best practices and coding standards, ensuring a consistent and maintainable codebase, even in large teams.

3. Responsiveness: Many frameworks are designed with responsiveness in mind, making it easier to create mobile-friendly and cross-browser-compatible applications.

4. State Management: Front-end frameworks often include tools for managing application state, which is crucial for building interactive web applications.

5. Community and Ecosystem: Frameworks usually have large communities, extensive documentation, and a rich ecosystem of plugins and extensions.

Popular Front-End Frameworks

Several popular front-end frameworks are widely used in the web development industry. Some of the most notable ones include:

1. React: Developed by Facebook, React is a JavaScript library for building user interfaces. It's known for its component-based architecture and is used by companies like Facebook, Instagram, and Airbnb.

2. Angular: Developed by Google, Angular is a comprehensive framework for building web and mobile applications. It provides features like two-way data binding and dependency injection.

3. Vue.js: A progressive JavaScript framework for building user interfaces. Vue is known for its simplicity and flexibility and is often compared to React and Angular.

Getting Started with a Front-End Framework

Let's take a brief look at how to get started with React, one of the popular front-end frameworks:

1. Installation: To start a React project, you can use Create React App, a tool that sets up a new React project with the necessary files and dependencies. Run the following command to create a new React app:

```bash
npx create-react-app my-app
```

2. Components: React applications are built using components. You can create a new component by defining a JavaScript function or class that returns JSX (JavaScript XML) to describe the component's UI.

```jsx
import React from 'react';

function App() {
  return (
    <div>
      <h1>Hello, React!</h1>
    </div>
  );
}
```

```jsx
export default App;
```

3. Rendering: You can render your React component by including it in your HTML file with a root element, often an empty `<div>` with an `id`.

```html
<div id="root"></div>
```

4. State and Props: React allows you to manage component state and pass data via props, enabling dynamic and interactive UIs.

```jsx
// Using state
import React, { useState } from 'react';

function Counter() {
  const [count, setCount] = useState(0);

  return (
    <div>
      <p>Count: {count}</p>
      <button onClick={() => setCount(count + 1)}>Increment</button>
    </div>
```

```
  );

}


export default Counter;

```
```

5. Building and Deployment: To build and deploy your React application, you can use tools like `npm` and services like Netlify, Vercel, or GitHub Pages.

Conclusion

Front-end frameworks are indispensable tools for modern web development. They offer efficiency, consistency, and enhanced capabilities for building web applications. In this section, we've introduced the concept of front-end frameworks and briefly explored React as an example. In the upcoming sections, we will dive deeper into specific aspects of front-end frameworks and their application in web development.
```

8.2 Popular JavaScript Frameworks (e.g., React, Angular, Vue.js)

In this section, we will explore some of the most popular front-end JavaScript frameworks and libraries: React, Angular, and Vue.js. Each of these frameworks has its strengths and use cases, and we will provide an overview of each, along with code examples to illustrate their key concepts.

1. React

Overview: React is a JavaScript library developed by Facebook for building user interfaces. It's known for its component-based architecture and its virtual DOM, which allows for efficient updates to the UI.

Key Concepts:

- **Components:** React applications are built using components. Components are reusable and encapsulate the UI and behavior.

- **Virtual DOM:** React uses a virtual DOM to efficiently update the actual DOM when data changes. This minimizes the number of direct DOM manipulations.

Example:

```jsx
import React from 'react';
```

```
class App extends React.Component {

 render() {

  return (

   <div>

    <h1>Hello, React!</h1>

   </div>

  );

 }

}


export default App;
```

```


2. Angular


**Overview:** Angular is a comprehensive front-end framework developed by Google. It provides a robust set of features for building web and mobile applications, including two-way data binding, dependency injection, and a powerful CLI.


**Key Concepts:**


- **Modules:** Angular applications are organized into modules, which encapsulate functionality.
```

- **Components:** Like React, Angular uses a component-based architecture for building UIs.

Example:

```typescript
import { Component } from '@angular/core';

@Component({
  selector: 'app-root',
  template: '<h1>Hello, Angular!</h1>',
})
export class AppComponent {}
```

3. Vue.js

Overview: Vue.js is a progressive JavaScript framework that's often compared to React and Angular. It's known for its simplicity and flexibility.

Key Concepts:

- **Vue Instance:** A Vue.js application starts with a Vue instance, which is responsible for the view model.

- Directives: Vue.js uses directives in the template to declaratively render dynamic content.

Example:

```html
<!DOCTYPE html>
<html>
 <head>
  <script src="https://cdn.jsdelivr.net/npm/vue@2.6.14/dist/vue.js"></script>
 </head>
 <body>
  <div id="app">
   <h1>{{ message }}</h1>
  </div>

  <script>
   var app = new Vue({
    el: '#app',
    data: {
     message: 'Hello, Vue!'
    }
   });
  </script>
```

```
  </body>

</html>

```
```

Choosing the Right Framework

- **React:** Great for building user interfaces, especially in single-page applications. It's highly popular and has a large community and ecosystem.

- **Angular:** Suitable for larger applications with complex requirements. It provides a full-featured framework for both web and mobile.

- **Vue.js:** Offers a middle-ground between React and Angular, providing flexibility and simplicity. It's a good choice for smaller to medium-sized applications.

Conclusion

Front-end development has been revolutionized by the introduction of JavaScript frameworks and libraries like React, Angular, and Vue.js. Each of these tools has its strengths and is suitable for different project requirements. In this section, we've provided an overview of these frameworks, along with code examples to illustrate their core concepts. Depending on your project's needs and your personal preferences, you can choose the framework that best suits your development goals.
```

8.3 Managing State in Web Applications

In this section, we will explore the crucial topic of managing state in web applications. State management is a fundamental aspect of building interactive and dynamic web applications. We will discuss various approaches to state management and provide code examples to illustrate these concepts.

What is State in a Web Application?

State in a web application refers to the data that represents the current condition or context of the application. This data can include user input, application settings, and other information that determines how the application behaves and presents information to the user.

Why Is State Management Important?

Effective state management is essential for the following reasons:

1. User Interactions: Web applications often involve complex user interactions and dynamic updates. Proper state management ensures that these interactions are handled correctly.

2. Data Persistence: State management allows you to preserve user data and application settings between page reloads or across different components.

3. Data Sharing: Components in a web application may need to share data with each other. State management provides a mechanism for sharing data between components.

4. Predictable Behavior: Well-structured state management leads to predictable application behavior, making it easier to debug and maintain.

Approaches to State Management

There are various approaches to managing state in web applications, including:

1. Local Component State: In many cases, state can be managed within individual components. This is suitable for small-scale applications or when the state is specific to a single component.

2. Prop Drilling: Passing state down through component props is another method, but it can become cumbersome in applications with deeply nested components.

3. State Management Libraries: For larger and more complex applications, state management libraries like Redux (for React), NgRx (for Angular), and Vuex (for Vue.js) can provide a centralized way to manage state.

Example of Local Component State (React)

Let's consider a simple example of managing local component state in a React application. We'll create a counter component that maintains its own state:

```jsx
import React, { useState } from 'react';

function Counter() {
```

```
// Initialize state with a count of 0

const [count, setCount] = useState(0);


const increment = () => {

  // Update the count state when the button is clicked

  setCount(count + 1);

};


return (

  <div>

    <p>Count: {count}</p>

    <button onClick={increment}>Increment</button>

  </div>

);

}


export default Counter;
```
```

**Example of State Management Library (Redux)**

For more complex applications, using a state management library like Redux can be beneficial. Redux centralizes application state in a store and provides actions and reducers to update and query that state.
```

```javascript
// Redux action
const increment = () => {
  return {
    type: 'INCREMENT',
  };
};

// Redux reducer
const counterReducer = (state = 0, action) => {
  switch (action.type) {
    case 'INCREMENT':
      return state + 1;
    default:
      return state;
  }
};

// Redux store
import { createStore } from 'redux';

const store = createStore(counterReducer);
```

```
// React component connected to Redux store
import React from 'react';
import { useSelector, useDispatch } from 'react-redux';

function Counter() {
  const count = useSelector((state) => state);
  const dispatch = useDispatch();

  const increment = () => {
    dispatch(increment());
  };

  return (
    <div>
      <p>Count: {count}</p>
      <button onClick={increment}>Increment</button>
    </div>
  );
}
```

Conclusion

Managing state in web applications is a critical aspect of building interactive and dynamic user experiences. Depending on the complexity of your application, you can use local component state, prop drilling, or state management libraries like Redux to handle state effectively. In this section, we've explored the importance of state management and provided examples of different approaches to get you started.

8.4 Component-Based Architecture

In this section, we will delve into the concept of component-based architecture in front-end development. Component-based architecture is a fundamental concept in modern web development, and it plays a central role in frameworks like React, Angular, and Vue.js. We will explore what component-based architecture is, why it's important, and how to implement it with code examples.

What is Component-Based Architecture?

Component-based architecture is a design approach that decomposes a user interface into smaller, self-contained, and reusable building blocks called components. Each component encapsulates a specific piece of functionality, user interface, or behavior, making it easier to develop, test, and maintain complex web applications.

Key Concepts of Component-Based Architecture

1. Reusability: Components are designed to be reusable across different parts of an application. This promotes a modular and efficient development process.

2. Encapsulation: Components encapsulate their internal logic and state, hiding implementation details from the outside world. This enhances code organization and separation of concerns.

3. Composition: Larger components can be built by combining smaller components. This allows developers to create complex user interfaces by composing simpler, well-defined parts.

4. Isolation: Components should ideally operate independently, reducing the risk of unintended side effects and making it easier to test and maintain the code.

Example of Component-Based Architecture (React)

Let's consider a simple example of component-based architecture in a React application. We'll create a basic "To-Do List" application with two components: `TodoApp` and `TodoItem`.

```jsx
// TodoItem.js
import React from 'react';

function TodoItem({ text, completed }) {
  return (
    <li style={{ textDecoration: completed ? 'line-through' : 'none' }}>
      {text}
    </li>
  );
}

export default TodoItem;

// TodoApp.js
import React, { useState } from 'react';
```

```
import TodoItem from './TodoItem';

function TodoApp() {
  const [todos, setTodos] = useState([]);
  const [input, setInput] = useState('');

  const addTodo = () => {
    setTodos([...todos, { text: input, completed: false }]);
    setInput('');
  };

  return (
    <div>
      <h1>Todo List</h1>
      <input
        type="text"
        value={input}
        onChange={(e) => setInput(e.target.value)}
      />
      <button onClick={addTodo}>Add</button>
      <ul>
        {todos.map((todo, index) => (
          <TodoItem key={index} text={todo.text} completed={todo.completed} />
```

```
    ))}
  </ul>
  </div>
 );
}


export default TodoApp;
```
```

In this example, we have two components: `TodoItem` and `TodoApp`. `TodoItem` represents an individual to-do item, and `TodoApp` represents the entire to-do list application. The `TodoApp` component uses `TodoItem` to render each to-do item in the list.

This illustrates how component-based architecture promotes reusability and encapsulation.

**Benefits of Component-Based Architecture**

**1. Reusability:** Components can be reused throughout an application, reducing code duplication.

**2. Maintainability:** Smaller, focused components are easier to understand, test, and maintain.

**3. Collaboration:** Different teams or developers can work on separate components simultaneously.
```

4. Scalability: As an application grows, components can be added, modified, or replaced without affecting the entire codebase.

Conclusion

Component-based architecture is a fundamental concept in modern front-end development. It promotes code reusability, encapsulation, and maintainability, making it easier to build and scale complex web applications. In this section, we've explored the key concepts of component-based architecture and provided a code example in React to illustrate its implementation.

8.5 Building Single-Page Applications (SPAs)

In this section, we will explore the concept of Single-Page Applications (SPAs) in web development. SPAs have become increasingly popular for building modern web applications, providing a smooth and responsive user experience. We will discuss what SPAs are, their benefits, and how to build one using a front-end framework.

What is a Single-Page Application (SPA)?

A Single-Page Application (SPA) is a type of web application that loads a single HTML page and dynamically updates its content as the user interacts with the app. SPAs aim to provide a seamless and fluid user experience by avoiding full-page reloads during navigation. Instead, they load data, update the URL, and modify the page's content dynamically.

Key Characteristics of SPAs

1. Single HTML Page: SPAs typically consist of a single HTML file that serves as the application's shell.

2. Client-Side Routing: SPAs use client-side routing to update the URL and display the appropriate content without making a full server request.

3. AJAX Requests: SPAs rely heavily on asynchronous requests (AJAX) to fetch data from the server as needed, often using APIs or JSON for data exchange.

4. Dynamic Updates: The content of an SPA is updated dynamically without requiring a full page reload, resulting in a smoother user experience.

5. State Management: SPAs often use client-side state management libraries to handle application state, ensuring that the UI remains in sync with the underlying data.

Benefits of SPAs

1. Fast and Responsive: SPAs offer a faster and more responsive user experience since they only update the parts of the page that change, reducing network requests.

2. Smooth Navigation: Users can navigate through an SPA without the interruptions of page refreshes, creating a more fluid experience.

3. Reduced Server Load: SPAs reduce the load on the server since most of the application logic and rendering are performed on the client side.

4. Offline Support: With proper caching and service workers, SPAs can work offline, providing users with access to content even when they're not connected to the internet.

Building an SPA with React

React is a popular choice for building SPAs due to its component-based architecture and efficient rendering. Here's a high-level overview of how to build an SPA with React:

1. Set Up Your Project: Create a new React project using a tool like Create React App or set up your development environment manually.

2. Create Components: Build individual components for different parts of your application, such as navigation bars, headers, content sections, and footers.

3. Implement Routing: Use a routing library like React Router to handle client-side routing. Define routes and map them to specific components.

4. Manage State: Choose a state management solution like Redux or the React Context API to manage global state, ensuring that your components can access and update data as needed.

5. Fetch Data: Use asynchronous requests (AJAX) to fetch data from your server or external APIs. Update your components with the retrieved data.

6. Optimize for Performance: Implement techniques like code splitting, lazy loading, and caching to optimize your SPA's performance.

7. Testing and Deployment: Write tests for your components and features, and then deploy your SPA to a hosting platform.

Here's a simplified example of how you can set up routing in a React SPA using React Router:

```jsx
import React from 'react';
import { BrowserRouter as Router, Route, Switch } from 'react-router-dom';
import Home from './components/Home';
import About from './components/About';
import Contact from './components/Contact';

function App() {
  return (
    <Router>
```

```
      <Switch>

        <Route exact path="/" component={Home} />

        <Route path="/about" component={About} />

        <Route path="/contact" component={Contact} />

      </Switch>

    </Router>

  );

}


export default App;

```
```

In this example, we've set up routing for a basic SPA with three pages: Home, About, and Contact.

Conclusion

Single-Page Applications (SPAs) offer a modern and responsive user experience by loading content dynamically and avoiding full page reloads. Building an SPA with a front-end framework like React allows you to create interactive and efficient web applications. In this section, we've explored the characteristics, benefits, and basic steps involved in building an SPA.
```

CHAPTER IX
Web Accessibility and Inclusive Design

9.1 Importance of Web Accessibility

In this section, we will delve into the critical topic of web accessibility and the significance of designing and developing websites and web applications that are inclusive and accessible to all users. We will discuss why web accessibility matters, its benefits, and how to get started with accessible web design.

What is Web Accessibility?

Web accessibility refers to the practice of making websites and web applications usable by people of all abilities, including those with disabilities. It ensures that individuals with disabilities can perceive, navigate, interact with, and contribute to the web. Web accessibility is not only about compliance with guidelines but also about creating an inclusive digital environment.

Why is Web Accessibility Important?

1. Inclusivity: Web accessibility ensures that everyone, regardless of their abilities, can access and use your digital content and services.

2. Legal Compliance: Many countries have laws and regulations that require websites and web applications to be accessible. Non-compliance can lead to legal consequences.

3. Broader Audience: An accessible website expands your potential audience to include individuals with disabilities, a sizable and diverse demographic.

4. Improved User Experience: Accessibility features often enhance the overall user experience for all users, such as captions in videos, clear navigation, and text-to-speech capabilities.

5. Search Engine Optimization (SEO): Accessibility practices can improve SEO, as search engines favor websites with well-structured, accessible content.

How to Prioritize Web Accessibility

1. Learn the Guidelines: Familiarize yourself with accessibility guidelines such as the Web Content Accessibility Guidelines (WCAG). These guidelines provide best practices for making web content accessible.

2. Use Semantic HTML: Employ semantic HTML elements to ensure proper document structure and meaningful content. For example, use `<button>` elements for buttons and `<h1>` to `<h6>` for headings.

3. Provide Alternative Text: Always include descriptive alt text for images so that screen readers can convey the content to users who cannot see the images.

4. Ensure Keyboard Navigation: Make sure all interactive elements and functionality are operable via keyboard input alone. Keyboard navigation is crucial for users with mobility impairments.

5. Test with Assistive Technologies: Use screen readers, voice recognition software, and other assistive technologies to test your website's accessibility. Identify and address any issues.

Benefits of Web Accessibility

1. Inclusivity: Accessible websites ensure that everyone can access information and services.

2. Legal Compliance: Complying with accessibility laws reduces the risk of legal action and associated costs.

3. Better Reputation: An accessible website demonstrates social responsibility and can enhance your organization's reputation.

4. Increased User Engagement: Improved usability benefits all users, leading to increased engagement and user satisfaction.

5. Broader Market Reach: Accessible websites reach a larger audience, potentially increasing your customer base.

Conclusion

Web accessibility is not only a legal requirement but also a moral and practical necessity. Creating accessible websites and web applications ensures that everyone, regardless of their abilities, can participate in the digital world. In this section, we've highlighted the importance of web accessibility, its benefits, and provided initial steps to begin your journey towards making the web a more inclusive place for all users.

9.2 Creating Accessible HTML

In this section, we will explore the fundamental principles of creating accessible HTML content. Ensuring that your HTML is accessible is the first step in making your website or web application inclusive to all users, including those with disabilities. We will discuss essential HTML accessibility elements, attributes, and best practices.

Semantic HTML and Accessibility

Semantic HTML elements play a crucial role in web accessibility. These elements provide meaning and structure to your content. Here are some essential semantic elements and how to use them:

1. Headings (`<h1>` to `<h6>`): Use headings to organize content hierarchically. `<h1>` is the highest level, representing the main heading, followed by `<h2>`, `<h3>`, and so on. Ensure a logical and consistent heading structure throughout your document.

2. Lists (`<ul>`, `<ol>`, `<li>`): Use unordered lists (`<ul>`) for lists without a specific order and ordered lists (`<ol>`) for ordered lists. Use list items (`<li>`) for each list item. Screen readers announce lists, helping users understand content organization.

3. Links (`<a>`): Provide descriptive link text that conveys the link's purpose. Avoid generic text like "click here" or "read more." Use the `title` attribute sparingly and ensure the link is distinguishable through color and underline.

4. Buttons (`<button>`) and Form Controls: Use `<button>` elements for interactive buttons. For form controls like inputs and selects, associate labels using the `for` attribute and `id`. Provide helpful instructions or hints using the `aria-label` or `aria-describedby` attributes.

5. Tables (`<table>`, `<th>`, `<td>`): Make data tables accessible by using the `<table>` element for tabular data. Use `<th>` for table headers and `<td>` for data cells. Associate headers with cells using `scope`, `headers`, or `id` and `headers` attributes.

Alternative Text for Images

Adding alternative text (alt text) to images is a critical accessibility practice, as it provides a textual description of the image for users who cannot see it. Here's how to add alt text to images:

```html
<img src="image.jpg" alt="A picturesque sunset over a calm lake with mountains in the background">
```

Ensure that alt text is concise, descriptive, and conveys the image's essential information. For decorative images, use an empty `alt` attribute (`alt=""`) to indicate that the image is purely decorative and does not convey content.

Semantic HTML5 Elements

HTML5 introduced several semantic elements that can enhance web accessibility. These include:

- `<header>`: Represents introductory content or a set of navigational links.

- `<nav>`: Represents a section of navigation links.

- `<main>`: Represents the primary content of the document.

- `<article>`: Represents a self-contained composition in a document, such as a blog post or news article.

- `<aside>`: Represents content that is tangentially related to the content around it.

- `<footer>`: Represents the footer of a section or page.

Using these elements appropriately helps screen readers and other assistive technologies better understand your page's structure.

ARIA (Accessible Rich Internet Applications) Roles and Attributes

The Accessible Rich Internet Applications (ARIA) specification provides roles and attributes to enhance the accessibility of dynamic content, such as web applications. Use ARIA roles and attributes to convey additional information to assistive technologies.

For example, to make a div act like a button, you can use ARIA roles and attributes:

```html
<div role="button" tabindex="0" aria-label="Open menu">Menu</div>
```

- `role="button"` informs assistive technologies that this element functions as a button.

- `tabindex="0"` makes the element focusable with the keyboard.

- `aria-label` provides a label for the button.

Conclusion

Creating accessible HTML content is the foundation of web accessibility. By using semantic HTML elements, providing alternative text for images, and leveraging ARIA roles and attributes when necessary, you can ensure that your web content is inclusive and usable by all users, regardless of their abilities. In this section, we've covered essential HTML accessibility practices and techniques to get you started on your journey toward creating more accessible web experiences.

9.3 Designing with Accessibility in Mind

In this section, we will explore the principles and best practices of designing web interfaces with accessibility in mind. It's essential to consider accessibility from the early stages of design to create inclusive digital experiences. We'll cover key concepts and provide practical guidance for designing accessible user interfaces.

Understand Your Audience

1. User Personas: Create user personas that include individuals with various disabilities. Consider their needs, preferences, and challenges when designing.

2. User Testing: Involve users with disabilities in usability testing. Gather feedback and insights to refine your design.

Color Contrast and Text Legibility

1. Color Contrast: Ensure sufficient color contrast between text and background elements. Use tools like the WebAIM Color Contrast Checker to verify contrast ratios.

2. Font Choices: Select legible and easy-to-read fonts. Avoid decorative fonts for body text. Sans-serif fonts are often more accessible.

Keyboard Accessibility

1. Keyboard Focus: Ensure that all interactive elements can be accessed and activated using only the keyboard. Use the `:focus` pseudo-class to style focused elements.

2. Skip Links: Implement "skip to content" links at the beginning of the page to allow keyboard users to bypass repetitive navigation menus.

Responsive and Flexible Layouts

1. Responsive Design: Create responsive layouts that adapt to different screen sizes and orientations. Test with screen readers to ensure content reflows logically.

2. Flexible Text Sizes: Avoid fixed font sizes. Allow users to adjust text size without breaking the layout.

Semantic HTML and ARIA

1. Semantic Elements: Use semantic HTML5 elements (e.g., `<nav>`, `<main>`, `<section>`) to provide clear document structure.

2. ARIA Landmarks: Implement ARIA landmark roles (`role="banner"`, `role="main"`, etc.) to convey the page's structure to screen readers.

Focus Styles and Interactive Elements

1. Focus Styles: Ensure interactive elements (links, buttons, form fields) have visible and distinctive focus styles to indicate keyboard focus.

2. Button Roles: Use `<button>` elements for clickable actions. If using non-button elements, apply `role="button"` and provide appropriate ARIA attributes.

Multimedia Accessibility

1. Transcripts and Captions: Provide transcripts for audio content and captions for videos. Ensure that multimedia content is accessible to users with hearing impairments.

2. Alternative Text: Include descriptive alternative text for images and provide audio descriptions for complex visuals in videos.

Testing with Real Users

1. User Testing: Conduct usability testing with individuals with disabilities. This helps identify design issues and gather valuable feedback.

2. Accessibility Tools: Use browser extensions and accessibility testing tools to evaluate your design for accessibility compliance.

Documentation and Training

1. Accessibility Guidelines: Create and maintain accessibility guidelines and documentation for your design team. Ensure that everyone understands their role in achieving accessibility goals.

2. Training: Provide training sessions on accessibility best practices for designers and developers to promote a culture of inclusion.

Conclusion

Designing with accessibility in mind is a crucial step towards creating digital experiences that are inclusive and usable by everyone. By understanding your audience, following best practices for color contrast, keyboard accessibility, semantic HTML, and multimedia accessibility, and involving users with disabilities in the design process, you can ensure that your web interfaces are welcoming to a diverse range of users. In this section, we've covered key principles and practical steps for integrating accessibility into your design workflow.

9.4 Testing and Auditing for Accessibility

In this section, we will delve into the crucial process of testing and auditing your web content for accessibility. Ensuring that your digital assets meet accessibility standards is essential for creating an inclusive online environment. We'll explore various testing methods and tools to help you identify and address accessibility issues.

Manual Testing

1. Keyboard Navigation: Navigate through your website using only the keyboard. Ensure all interactive elements are accessible and usable.

2. Screen Reader Testing: Use screen reader software (e.g., JAWS, NVDA, VoiceOver) to evaluate how content is presented to users who rely on auditory output.

3. Voice Commands: Test your web application using voice commands and ensure that all functions are accessible and respond to voice input.

4. High-Contrast Mode: Enable high-contrast mode on your operating system to check if your website remains legible and usable.

5. Zoom and Text Resizing: Test how your website responds to text resizing and zooming in different browsers.

Automated Testing

1. Accessibility Testing Tools: Utilize automated accessibility testing tools like Axe, Wave, or Lighthouse to scan your web pages for common issues. These tools can highlight problems such as missing alt text, color contrast violations, and structural issues.

2. Browser Developer Tools: Modern browsers have built-in accessibility auditing features. Use browser developer tools to check for accessibility violations and examine accessibility tree structures.

Validation and Compliance

1. HTML Validation: Ensure your HTML markup is well-formed and valid. Use HTML validators to check for syntax errors.

2. WCAG Compliance: Evaluate your content against the Web Content Accessibility Guidelines (WCAG) to ensure compliance with accessibility standards. WCAG provides specific criteria for accessibility levels (A, AA, AAA).

User Testing

1. Involving Users with Disabilities: Conduct user testing sessions with individuals who have various disabilities. Gather their feedback and insights on the accessibility of your web content.

2. Usability Testing: Combine accessibility testing with general usability testing to ensure that your website is both accessible and user-friendly.

Accessibility Audits

1. Comprehensive Audits: Consider hiring an accessibility expert or consultant to perform a detailed accessibility audit of your website. They can identify and document issues comprehensively.

2. Regular Audits: Schedule regular accessibility audits to catch new issues that may arise as you update your web content.

Documentation and Remediation

1. Issue Tracking: Document identified accessibility issues, including their severity and location in your content.

2. Prioritization: Prioritize issues based on their impact and complexity, focusing on critical problems that affect a large number of users.

3. Remediation: Implement fixes for identified issues and test them thoroughly to ensure they do not introduce new problems.

Accessibility Statements

1. Accessibility Statements: Create and publish an accessibility statement on your website, outlining your commitment to accessibility and providing contact information for users to report issues.

Continuous Improvement

1. Feedback Loop: Establish a feedback mechanism for users to report accessibility problems and improvements. Act on user feedback promptly.

2. Training: Provide ongoing training for your development and content teams to keep them updated on accessibility best practices and standards.

Conclusion

Testing and auditing for accessibility is an ongoing process that ensures your web content remains inclusive and usable for all users. By combining manual and automated testing methods, involving users with disabilities, and performing regular audits, you can identify and address accessibility issues effectively. Continuous improvement and a commitment to accessibility will help you create a web environment that is welcoming and accessible to everyone. In this section, we've explored various testing methods and tools to help you achieve this goal.

9.5 Assistive Technologies and User Testing

In this section, we will explore assistive technologies and how to conduct user testing with individuals who rely on these tools to access digital content. Understanding how assistive technologies work and involving users with disabilities in testing is essential for creating truly inclusive and accessible web experiences.

Understanding Assistive Technologies

1. Screen Readers: Learn about screen reader software such as JAWS, NVDA, and VoiceOver, which provide auditory output of digital content to users who are blind or visually impaired.

2. Braille Displays: Explore Braille displays that convert digital content into Braille text, allowing users with visual impairments to read through touch.

3. Screen Magnifiers: Understand screen magnification software that helps users with low vision by enlarging content on the screen.

4. Voice Recognition Software: Familiarize yourself with voice recognition tools like Dragon NaturallySpeaking, which enable users with mobility impairments to control computers and dictate text.

5. Keyboard Navigation: Learn how users with mobility impairments navigate web content using keyboards and keyboard shortcuts.

User Testing with Assistive Technologies

1. Recruiting Participants: Identify and recruit individuals with disabilities who use assistive technologies for user testing. Consider various disabilities, including visual, auditory, and motor impairments.

2. Creating Test Scenarios: Develop test scenarios that reflect common user tasks on your website or application. Ensure these scenarios cover a range of functionalities.

3. Providing Assistive Technologies: Make sure you have the necessary assistive technologies and devices available for participants during testing.

4. Observing Interactions: Observe how participants interact with your digital content using assistive technologies. Pay attention to any difficulties or challenges they encounter.

5. Gathering Feedback: Collect feedback from participants about their user experience, including barriers they encountered and suggestions for improvement.

Accessibility Testing Tools

1. Screen Reader Emulators: Use screen reader emulators or browser extensions to simulate screen reader interactions during testing. These tools help you experience your content as a user with visual impairments would.

2. Keyboard Emulators: Emulate keyboard-only navigation to identify keyboard accessibility issues and ensure that all interactive elements are reachable and usable.

3. Color Contrast Analyzers: Employ color contrast analyzers to check the legibility of your content for users with visual impairments.

Real-World Examples

Let's walk through a real-world example of conducting user testing with assistive technologies:

Scenario: Testing the accessibility of an e-commerce website for blind users.

1. Recruitment: Identify blind users who rely on screen readers for the test. Ensure a diverse group of participants.

2. Test Tasks: Create tasks such as browsing product listings, adding items to the cart, and completing a purchase.

3. Observation: Observe how participants navigate the website using screen readers. Take note of any issues with content structure, keyboard accessibility, or form inputs.

4. Feedback: Gather feedback from participants about their experience. Ask them to describe any challenges they encountered and suggest improvements.

5. Iterative Testing: Use the feedback to make improvements to the website's accessibility and repeat the testing process to verify the changes.

Conclusion

Understanding assistive technologies and involving users who rely on them in testing is a critical step in ensuring the accessibility of your digital content. By experiencing your website or application from their perspective, you can identify and address accessibility barriers effectively. In this section, we've explored the key concepts and practices related to assistive technologies and user testing, helping you create more inclusive web experiences for all users.

CHAPTER X
Cross-Browser Compatibility

10.1 Dealing with Browser Differences

In this section, we will explore the challenges of cross-browser compatibility and provide strategies and techniques for dealing with browser differences effectively. Ensuring that your web application functions consistently across various browsers is crucial for providing a seamless user experience.

Understanding Browser Differences

1. Browser Ecosystem: Recognize that there are multiple web browsers, each with its rendering engine and quirks. Popular browsers include Chrome, Firefox, Safari, Edge, and Internet Explorer (for legacy support).

2. Rendering Engines: Learn about the rendering engines that browsers use, such as Blink (used by Chrome), Gecko (used by Firefox), WebKit (used by Safari), and EdgeHTML (used by older versions of Edge).

3. Version Variations: Be aware that different browser versions may have varying levels of support for web standards and features. Older browsers may lack support for modern HTML5 and CSS3 features.

Strategies for Handling Browser Differences

1. Feature Detection: Embrace feature detection techniques to check if a specific browser supports a feature before using it. This approach helps you avoid using unsupported features and provides graceful fallbacks.

2. User Agent Sniffing: Understand the concept of user agent sniffing but use it sparingly. User agent strings can be unreliable and can lead to incorrect assumptions about a browser's capabilities.

3. Progressive Enhancement: Implement a progressive enhancement strategy, where you start with a basic, functional version of your web application and then enhance it with features that are supported by the user's browser.

4. Graceful Degradation: Employ graceful degradation, which involves building your web application with all modern features and then ensuring that it functions adequately in older or less-capable browsers.

5. Polyfills: Utilize polyfills, which are JavaScript libraries that provide modern functionality to older browsers that lack support. Polyfills can bridge the gap by adding missing features.

Cross-Browser CSS

1. Vendor Prefixes: Learn how to use vendor prefixes (-webkit-, -moz-, -ms-, -o-) to target specific browser implementations of CSS properties. Understand when and how to apply them.

2. CSS Resets and Normalization: Explore CSS resets and normalization techniques to ensure consistent styling across different browsers. These tools help you establish a baseline styling foundation.

JavaScript Considerations

1. ES6 and Transpilers: Be aware of ES6 (ECMAScript 2015) features and use transpilers like Babel to convert modern JavaScript into a compatible version for older browsers.

2. Browser Compatibility Tables: Refer to browser compatibility tables and resources (e.g., MDN Web Docs) to check the support status of specific JavaScript methods and APIs in various browsers.

Real-World Example

Let's walk through a real-world example of dealing with browser differences:

Scenario: Implementing a responsive image gallery that relies on the `object-fit` CSS property, which is not supported in older versions of Internet Explorer (IE).

1. Feature Detection: Use feature detection to check if the browser supports `object-fit` by detecting the presence of the property using JavaScript.

2. Polyfill: If `object-fit` is not supported, apply a polyfill that replicates the functionality using JavaScript and CSS, ensuring that the gallery remains functional in older IE versions.

3. Graceful Degradation: Ensure that even in browsers without `object-fit` support, the gallery still displays images without distortion, even if it lacks the desired styling.

Conclusion

Dealing with browser differences is an ongoing challenge in web development. By understanding the browser ecosystem, employing strategies like feature detection and progressive enhancement, and using tools like polyfills and vendor prefixes, you can create web applications that work seamlessly across a wide range of browsers. In this section, we've explored these strategies and provided guidance on handling browser differences effectively.

10.2 Feature Detection vs. User Agent Sniffing

In this section, we will dive deep into the two primary methods used to handle browser differences: Feature Detection and User Agent Sniffing. Understanding when and how to use each approach is crucial for ensuring cross-browser compatibility in your web applications.

Feature Detection

What is Feature Detection?

Feature detection is a JavaScript technique used to check whether a particular feature or capability is supported by the user's web browser before using it. This approach is considered the best practice for handling cross-browser compatibility.

How to Perform Feature Detection

1. Select the Feature: Identify the feature or functionality you want to use in your web application. For example, you might want to check if the browser supports the HTML5 `<canvas>` element.

2. Write a Detection Script: Create a JavaScript script that tests for the presence of the feature. Here's an example of feature detection for the `<canvas>` element:

```javascript
if (typeof document.createElement('canvas').getContext === 'function') {
  // The browser supports the <canvas> element and its 2D context.
```

```
    // You can safely use it in your application.

} else {

    // The browser does not support the <canvas> element.

    // Provide a fallback or alternative functionality.

}
```
```

**3. Provide a Fallback:** In the case where the feature is not supported, it's essential to have a fallback or alternative functionality in place to ensure that the application remains usable.

**Advantages of Feature Detection**

- Reliable: Feature detection is based on actual browser capabilities, making it a reliable method for cross-browser compatibility.

- Graceful Degradation: It allows for graceful degradation, where the application can provide an alternative experience for unsupported browsers.

**User Agent Sniffing**

**What is User Agent Sniffing?**

User agent sniffing involves examining the user agent string provided by the browser to identify its make, version, and other details. While this method was once common, it's now generally discouraged due to its limitations and potential inaccuracies.
```

How to Perform User Agent Sniffing

1. Access the User Agent String: Retrieve the user agent string using JavaScript. This string contains information about the browser.

```javascript
var userAgent = navigator.userAgent;
```

2. Analyze the User Agent: Parse and analyze the user agent string to determine the browser type and version. For example, you might look for specific keywords or patterns in the user agent string.

3. Apply Browser-Specific Code: Based on the browser identification, you can execute browser-specific code or workarounds. Here's a simplified example:

```javascript
if (userAgent.indexOf("Chrome") !== -1) {
  // This code is for Chrome.
} else if (userAgent.indexOf("Firefox") !== -1) {
  // This code is for Firefox.
} else {
  // Fallback code for other browsers.
}
```

Drawbacks of User Agent Sniffing

- Fragile: User agent strings can be manipulated or spoofed, leading to incorrect browser identification.

- Maintenance: Browser updates and changes in user agent strings make maintenance challenging.

Choosing Between Feature Detection and User Agent Sniffing

In most cases, feature detection is the preferred method for handling browser differences. It is more reliable, future-proof, and aligns with best practices in web development.

Use user agent sniffing as a last resort when dealing with specific situations where feature detection is not feasible, and you have no other options. Even in such cases, exercise caution and be aware of its limitations.

Real-World Example

Let's explore a real-world scenario:

Scenario: You want to use the `localStorage` API in your web application. However, you're aware that some older browsers, such as Internet Explorer 7, do not support it.

Feature Detection Approach:

```javascript
if ('localStorage' in window && window['localStorage'] !== null) {

  // The browser supports the localStorage API.

  // You can safely use it in your application.

} else {

  // Provide a fallback or alternative functionality for browsers that do not support localStorage.

}
```

User Agent Sniffing Approach:

```javascript
var userAgent = navigator.userAgent;


if (userAgent.indexOf("MSIE 7.0") !== -1) {

  // This code is for Internet Explorer 7.

} else {

  // Code for other browsers.

}
```

In this example, the feature detection approach is more robust and recommended for determining support for `localStorage`. It checks the actual feature availability and ensures a more reliable cross-browser experience.

Conclusion

Feature detection is the preferred method for handling browser differences because it is more reliable, flexible, and aligns with best practices. User agent sniffing should only be used as a last resort when no other options are available. By understanding the differences between these approaches, you can ensure better cross-browser compatibility for your web applications.

10.3 Polyfills and Vendor Prefixes

In this section, we will explore the use of polyfills and vendor prefixes as strategies to address cross-browser compatibility issues in web development.

Polyfills

What are Polyfills?

Polyfills are JavaScript code snippets or libraries that provide modern web features to older browsers that lack support for those features. They allow developers to write code using the latest web standards while ensuring compatibility with older browser versions.

When to Use Polyfills

You should consider using polyfills in the following situations:

1. Missing HTML5/CSS3 Features: When you need to use HTML5 or CSS3 features that are not supported in older browsers (e.g., `<canvas>` element, CSS Flexbox, or CSS Grid).

2. JavaScript APIs: When you want to use modern JavaScript APIs that are not available in older browsers (e.g., `fetch()` for network requests or `localStorage` for data storage).

3. Consistency: When you want to maintain a consistent user experience across all browsers.

How to Use Polyfills

Here's a step-by-step guide on how to use polyfills:

1. Identify the Missing Feature: Determine which feature or API is not supported in the target browsers.

2. Choose a Polyfill: Search for an appropriate polyfill library or script that provides support for the missing feature. Several popular polyfill libraries include Babel, Polyfill.io, and Modernizr.

3. Include the Polyfill: Add the polyfill script to your HTML document using a `<script>` tag. It's essential to include it before your JavaScript code that relies on the missing feature.

```html
<script src="polyfill.js"></script>
<script src="your-script.js"></script>
```

4. Use the Feature: Write your JavaScript or CSS code as if the feature is universally supported, knowing that the polyfill will provide the necessary functionality for older browsers.

5. Test Thoroughly: Test your application in various browsers to ensure that the polyfill works as expected. Consider using cross-browser testing tools to streamline this process.

Vendor Prefixes

What are Vendor Prefixes?

Vendor prefixes are short codes or prefixes added to CSS properties to specify which browser engine should use a particular experimental CSS feature. They were commonly used in the past to implement features before they were standardized.

When to Use Vendor Prefixes

Vendor prefixes should be used cautiously and primarily for experimental or non-standardized features. However, in modern web development, they are becoming less necessary because most browsers now support standard CSS properties.

How to Use Vendor Prefixes

Here's how to use vendor prefixes when working with CSS:

1. Identify the Feature: Determine if the CSS property or feature you intend to use requires a vendor prefix. You can check CSS documentation or online resources to find out which properties need prefixes.

2. Apply the Prefix: Add the appropriate vendor prefix before the CSS property you want to use. Each browser engine has its prefix:

  - WebKit (Safari, Chrome): `-webkit-`

  - Mozilla (Firefox): `-moz-`

- Microsoft (Internet Explorer, Edge): `-ms-`

- Opera: `-o-`

For example, if you want to use the `transition` property with a WebKit prefix:

```css
.element {
  -webkit-transition: opacity 0.5s;
  transition: opacity 0.5s; /* Standard property */
}
```

3. Include the Standard Property: Always include the standard, non-prefixed property alongside vendor-prefixed versions. This ensures compatibility with modern browsers that no longer require prefixes.

4. Test Across Browsers: Test your CSS in various browsers to ensure that the prefixed properties work as expected. Use browser developer tools to debug and verify compatibility.

Conclusion

Polyfills and vendor prefixes are essential tools for addressing cross-browser compatibility issues in web development. Polyfills enable you to provide missing features to older browsers, while vendor prefixes help you implement experimental CSS features. However, it's essential to use these techniques judiciously, keeping in mind the changing landscape of web standards and the decreasing need for prefixes in modern web development. Always test thoroughly across different browsers to ensure a consistent and reliable user experience.

10.4 Cross-Browser Testing Tools and Services

In this section, we will explore various cross-browser testing tools and services that help web developers ensure their websites work consistently across different browsers and platforms.

Why Cross-Browser Testing is Crucial

Cross-browser testing is essential because web developers need to ensure that their websites or web applications function correctly and appear consistently across a wide range of browsers and devices. Each browser has its rendering engine, which may interpret HTML, CSS, and JavaScript differently. Additionally, users access the web from various devices, such as desktop computers, laptops, tablets, and smartphones, each with its screen size and capabilities.

By performing cross-browser testing, developers can identify and fix compatibility issues early in the development process, resulting in a better user experience and increased accessibility for all users.

Cross-Browser Testing Tools

Here are some popular cross-browser testing tools and services:

1. BrowserStack:

   - BrowserStack is a cloud-based cross-browser testing platform that allows developers to test their websites on a wide range of browsers and devices.

   - It provides real-time interactive testing, automated screenshot testing, and even access to preinstalled developer tools in browsers.

   - BrowserStack integrates with popular development and testing tools like Selenium, Appium, and JIRA.

2. Sauce Labs:

  - Sauce Labs is another cloud-based testing platform that offers cross-browser and cross-device testing.

  - It supports automated testing for web and mobile applications, making it suitable for testing on both desktop and mobile browsers.

  - Sauce Labs provides extensive testing environments and integrations with various testing frameworks.

3. CrossBrowserTesting:

  - CrossBrowserTesting is a cloud-based testing tool that offers manual and automated testing on a wide range of browsers and devices.

  - It provides access to real devices and emulators for mobile testing.

  - Developers can use CrossBrowserTesting to run Selenium and Appium scripts.

4. LambdaTest:

  - LambdaTest is a cloud-based platform that offers cross-browser testing with a focus on speed and scalability.

  - It provides real-time interactive testing, automated screenshot testing, and seamless integration with popular tools like JIRA and Slack.

How to Perform Cross-Browser Testing

Performing cross-browser testing typically involves the following steps:

1. Identify Target Browsers: Determine which browsers and browser versions your website or web application should support. Consider the browsers used by your target audience.

2. Select a Testing Tool: Choose a cross-browser testing tool or service that suits your needs. The tools mentioned above offer various features and pricing plans, so select the one that aligns with your project requirements.

3. Create Test Cases: Develop a set of test cases that cover the critical functionality of your website or application. These test cases should include scenarios specific to different browsers and devices.

4. Execute Tests: Use the selected testing tool to execute your test cases on the chosen browsers and devices. This may involve manual testing or automated testing using testing scripts.

5. Analyze Results: Carefully review the test results. Identify any issues, discrepancies, or visual inconsistencies that may have surfaced during testing.

6. Debug and Fix: If issues are detected, debug and fix them. Depending on the severity of the problem, you may need to modify your code, adjust CSS styles, or implement specific workarounds for problematic browsers.

7. Retest: After making fixes, re-run the tests to ensure that the issues have been resolved without introducing new problems.

8. Repeat as Necessary: Continue to test and retest on different browsers and devices as needed throughout the development process and after any significant updates.

Conclusion

Cross-browser testing is a crucial step in web development to ensure that your website or web application functions as intended across various browsers and devices. By leveraging cross-browser testing tools and services, developers can streamline the testing process and deliver a consistent user experience to a broad audience. Remember to test early and often to catch compatibility issues and address them proactively.

CHAPTER XI
Trends in Front-End Development

11.1 Progressive Web Apps (PWAs)

Progressive Web Apps (PWAs) are a modern approach to building web applications that provide a native app-like experience on the web. They combine the best of both web and mobile app worlds, offering enhanced performance, offline capabilities, and a responsive design. In this section, we will delve into what PWAs are, why they are essential, and how to create one step by step.

What is a Progressive Web App (PWA)?

A Progressive Web App is a web application that takes advantage of modern web technologies to deliver an app-like experience to users. PWAs are designed to work seamlessly on any platform or device with a web browser. They are called "progressive" because they progressively enhance the user experience based on the capabilities of the user's device and browser.

Key characteristics of PWAs include:

1. Progressive Enhancement: PWAs are built with progressive enhancement in mind, meaning they work for all users, regardless of the browser or device they are using. They enhance the experience for users with modern browsers and devices.

2. Responsive Design: PWAs are designed to adapt to different screen sizes and orientations, making them accessible on both desktop and mobile devices.

3. Offline Capabilities: PWAs can work offline or with a limited internet connection. This is achieved through the use of service workers, which cache essential assets and data.

4. App-like Experience: PWAs offer an app-like user experience, including smooth animations, fast loading times, and interactions that feel natural.

5. Secure: PWAs are served over HTTPS to ensure data privacy and security.

6. Discoverable: PWAs are discoverable by search engines, making them easy to find. They can also be added to the user's home screen, just like native apps.

Benefits of Progressive Web Apps

PWAs offer several advantages for both developers and users:

1. Improved Performance: PWAs are known for their fast load times and smooth interactions, leading to a better user experience.

2. Offline Functionality: Users can continue to use PWAs even when they are offline or have a weak internet connection.

3. Cross-Platform Compatibility: PWAs work on various platforms and devices, reducing the need for platform-specific development.

4. Reduced Development Costs: Building a single PWA that works across platforms can be more cost-effective than developing separate native apps for each platform.

5. Easier Updates: Developers can push updates to PWAs without requiring users to download and install new versions.

How to Create a Progressive Web App

Creating a PWA involves several key steps:

1. Set Up a Secure HTTPS Server: PWAs require a secure connection. Ensure your website is served over HTTPS.

2. Create a Manifest File: Create a manifest file (usually named `manifest.json`) that includes metadata about your app, such as its name, icons, and color scheme.

3. Implement Service Workers: Service workers are JavaScript files that act as a proxy between your app and the network. They enable offline functionality and caching. Implement service workers to cache essential assets and data.

4. Make the App Installable: Add a web app manifest to make your PWA installable. This allows users to add your app to their home screens.

5. Optimize for Performance: Optimize your PWA for performance by minimizing load times, using responsive design, and optimizing images and other assets.

6. Test Across Browsers: Test your PWA on various browsers and devices to ensure compatibility.

7. Promote Your PWA: Encourage users to install your PWA by displaying a "Add to Home Screen" prompt.

8. Monitor and Update: Continuously monitor your PWA's performance and user feedback. Update it as needed to improve the user experience.

Conclusion

Progressive Web Apps are a significant trend in front-end development, offering a user-friendly, cross-platform solution that combines the best of web and mobile app experiences. By following best practices and utilizing modern web technologies, developers can create PWAs that are fast, reliable, and accessible to a broad audience. PWAs represent the future of web development, providing a compelling alternative to traditional native apps.

11.2 Serverless Front-End

Serverless front-end development is an innovative approach that enables developers to build web applications without the traditional server infrastructure management. In this section, we'll explore what serverless front-end is, its benefits, and how to create a serverless front-end application step by step.

What is Serverless Front-End?

Serverless front-end, often referred to as "frontend as a service" or FaaS, is a development approach that shifts the responsibility of managing servers and infrastructure from developers to cloud providers. With serverless front-end, developers can focus solely on writing code for the client-side of their applications, leaving the backend, server provisioning, and scaling to the cloud platform.

Key characteristics of serverless front-end development include:

1. No Server Management: Developers are freed from managing servers, scaling, and infrastructure maintenance.

2. Microservices Architecture: Serverless front-end applications are often built using microservices, with each function or feature implemented as an independent service.

3. Auto-scaling: Cloud providers handle the scaling of resources automatically based on demand.

4. Pay-as-You-Go Pricing: Developers are billed only for the actual resources and execution time used, resulting in cost savings.

Benefits of Serverless Front-End

Serverless front-end development offers several advantages:

1. Cost-Efficiency: Developers don't need to pay for idle server time, reducing infrastructure costs.

2. Scalability: Applications can scale effortlessly with increasing demand without manual intervention.

3. Faster Development: Developers can focus on writing code rather than managing servers, speeding up development cycles.

4. Reduced Complexity: The serverless architecture simplifies infrastructure management, making it accessible to a broader range of developers.

5. Easy Maintenance: Cloud providers handle server maintenance, ensuring high availability and reliability.

How to Create a Serverless Front-End Application

Creating a serverless front-end application involves several key steps:

1. Select a Cloud Provider: Choose a cloud provider that offers serverless functions, such as AWS Lambda, Google Cloud Functions, or Azure Functions.

2. Design Your Architecture: Plan your application's architecture, defining the functions and microservices you need.

3. Develop Functions: Write serverless functions to handle specific tasks or features of your application. These functions should be stateless and independent.

4. Set Up APIs: Create APIs or endpoints for your functions to communicate with the frontend.

5. Frontend Development: Develop the frontend of your application using HTML, CSS, and JavaScript. Use AJAX or Fetch API to interact with the serverless functions.

6. Testing: Test your application thoroughly, including both the frontend and serverless functions.

7. Deployment: Deploy your frontend code to a content delivery network (CDN) or static hosting service. Deploy your serverless functions to your chosen cloud provider.

8. Monitoring and Maintenance: Set up monitoring and logging for your serverless functions to ensure they are running smoothly. Continuously monitor your application's performance.

Conclusion

Serverless front-end development is a forward-looking approach that simplifies infrastructure management, reduces costs, and accelerates development cycles. By leveraging cloud providers' serverless offerings, developers can focus on building the client-side of their applications and leave the backend complexities to the cloud platform. This trend in front-end development is gaining traction and has the potential to reshape how web applications are built and maintained.

11.3 WebAssembly and Its Applications

WebAssembly, often abbreviated as WASM, is a revolutionary technology that allows developers to run high-performance code written in languages other than JavaScript directly in web browsers. In this section, we'll explore what WebAssembly is, why it's a game-changer for web development, and how to use it in practical applications.

What is WebAssembly?

WebAssembly is a binary instruction format designed as a portable target for the compilation of high-level programming languages like C, C++, Rust, and others. It's supported by all major web browsers, including Chrome, Firefox, Safari, and Edge. WebAssembly code runs at near-native speed and provides a secure execution environment within web browsers.

Key features of WebAssembly include:

1. Performance: WebAssembly executes code at near-native speed, making it suitable for computationally intensive tasks.

2. Cross-Browser Compatibility: It's supported by all major browsers, ensuring broad compatibility.

3. Language Agnostic: Developers can write code in multiple languages and compile it to WebAssembly, expanding the choices beyond JavaScript.

4. Safe and Secure: WebAssembly runs in a sandboxed environment, preventing it from accessing sensitive browser APIs directly.

5. Compact and Efficient: WebAssembly binaries are compact and load quickly, improving web page load times.

Why WebAssembly is Important

WebAssembly is a game-changer for web development for several reasons:

1. Performance: It allows developers to build high-performance web applications, even for tasks that were previously reserved for native applications.

2. Language Freedom: WebAssembly opens the door to a wider range of programming languages for web development, enabling developers to choose the language that best suits their needs.

3. Reusability: Developers can reuse existing codebases written in other languages, reducing development time and effort.

4. Broad Compatibility: WebAssembly is supported across all major browsers, ensuring a consistent user experience.

Practical Applications of WebAssembly

WebAssembly has a wide range of applications, including:

1. Gaming: WebAssembly is suitable for building complex browser-based games with near-native performance.

2. Video and Audio Processing: It can be used for real-time video and audio processing, such as video editing or voice recognition.

3. Cryptocurrency and Blockchain: Many blockchain-based applications benefit from the performance and security of WebAssembly.

4. CAD and 3D Modeling: WebAssembly enables the development of web-based Computer-Aided Design (CAD) and 3D modeling applications.

How to Use WebAssembly in Your Projects

To use WebAssembly in your web projects, follow these steps:

1. Choose a Language: Select a language that compiles to WebAssembly, such as C, C++, or Rust.

2. Write Code: Write your code in the chosen language, ensuring it's compatible with WebAssembly.

3. Compile: Use a compiler or toolchain to compile your code into WebAssembly bytecode (WASM).

4. Load and Execute: In your web application, load the WASM file and use JavaScript to interact with it.

Here's a simplified example of using WebAssembly to calculate the Fibonacci sequence in C++:

```cpp
// Fibonacci.cpp
extern "C" {
   int fibonacci(int n) {
      if (n <= 2) return 1;
      return fibonacci(n - 1) + fibonacci(n - 2);
   }
}
```

Compile it to WASM:

```sh
emcc -O3 -s WASM=1 -o fibonacci.js Fibonacci.cpp
```

Then, in your JavaScript:

```javascript
```

```
const { fibonacci } = require('./fibonacci');


console.log(fibonacci(10)); // Output: 55
```

Conclusion

WebAssembly is a game-changing technology that enhances web development by offering high performance and language flexibility. Developers can leverage WebAssembly to bring computationally intensive tasks, games, and applications previously reserved for native platforms to the web. As browser support and tooling continue to evolve, the adoption of WebAssembly is expected to grow, making it a crucial trend in front-end development.

11.4 Web Components and Micro Frontends

In this section, we will delve into two significant trends in front-end development: Web Components and Micro Frontends. These technologies are transforming the way we build web applications by enabling modularity, reusability, and scalability.

Web Components: Building Blocks for Modern Web Development

Introduction to Web Components

Web Components are a set of web standards that allow developers to create reusable and encapsulated custom HTML elements. They consist of four main technologies:

1. Custom Elements: These enable developers to define their own HTML elements with custom behavior and properties.

2. Shadow DOM: Shadow DOM provides scoped styling and encapsulation for web components, preventing CSS and JavaScript conflicts.

3. HTML Templates: HTML templates allow you to declare fragments of markup that can be reused across your application.

4. HTML Imports: Although HTML Imports have been deprecated, the concept of importing and reusing web components remains a fundamental part of the Web Components ecosystem.

Benefits of Web Components

- **Reusability:** Web Components are self-contained and can be reused across different projects and frameworks.

- **Encapsulation:** The Shadow DOM ensures that the styles and behavior of a web component are encapsulated, preventing conflicts with the rest of the page.

- **Modularity:** You can break down your user interface into smaller, manageable components, enhancing maintainability.

- **Interoperability:** Web Components work well with various front-end libraries and frameworks.

Creating a Web Component

Let's create a simple "Hello World" web component:

```javascript
class HelloWorld extends HTMLElement {
  constructor() {
    super();
    this.attachShadow({ mode: 'open' });
  }

  connectedCallback() {
    this.shadowRoot.innerHTML = `<h1>Hello, <slot></slot>!</h1>`;
  }
```

}

```
customElements.define('hello-world', HelloWorld);
```

In this example:

- We create a `HelloWorld` class that extends `HTMLElement`.

- In the `constructor`, we attach a Shadow DOM to the custom element.

- In the `connectedCallback` method, we define the component's content using HTML templates and slots.

- Finally, we register the `hello-world` custom element using `customElements.define`.

You can use this component in your HTML like this:

```html
<hello-world>John</hello-world>
```

Micro Frontends: Building Scalable Web Applications

Introduction to Micro Frontends

Micro Frontends is an architectural approach that extends the concept of microservices to the front-end development. It involves breaking down a monolithic front-end into smaller, more manageable pieces, each with its own development team, technologies, and release cycles.

Benefits of Micro Frontends

- **Scalability:** Micro Frontends allow teams to work independently, making it easier to scale your development efforts.

- **Technological Diversity:** You can use different technologies and frameworks for each micro frontend, enabling flexibility and innovation.

- **Easier Maintenance:** Smaller codebases are easier to maintain and update.

- **Improved Collaboration:** Cross-functional teams can work on different parts of the application simultaneously.

Implementing Micro Frontends

Implementing Micro Frontends involves defining boundaries between different parts of your application, choosing appropriate communication mechanisms (e.g., APIs, events), and ensuring a consistent user experience.

Here's a simplified example of how you might structure a micro frontend application:

- **Container:** The main application shell that orchestrates the micro frontends.

- **Micro Frontend 1:** One of the independently developed and deployed parts of the application.

- **Micro Frontend 2:** Another micro frontend with its own codebase and team.

```html
<!-- Container (main application shell) -->
<div id="container">
  <!-- Micro Frontend 1 -->
  <div id="micro-frontend-1"></div>
  <!-- Micro Frontend 2 -->
  <div id="micro-frontend-2"></div>
</div>
```

In this example, the container can use techniques like iframe embedding, server-side composition, or client-side routing to integrate the micro frontends into the main application.

Conclusion

Web Components and Micro Frontends are two powerful trends in front-end development that address the challenges of building modern web applications. Web Components promote reusability and encapsulation, while Micro Frontends enable scalability and flexibility in large development teams. By incorporating these technologies into your front-end development toolbox, you can stay ahead in the ever-evolving landscape of web development.

11.5 The Future of Front-End Development

The field of front-end development is constantly evolving, driven by technological advancements and changing user expectations. In this section, we'll explore some of the emerging trends and predictions for the future of front-end development.

WebAssembly (Wasm): A Game-Changer for Web Applications

Introduction to WebAssembly

WebAssembly (Wasm) is a binary instruction format that enables high-performance execution of code on web browsers. It is designed to run at near-native speed and is supported by all major browsers. While initially conceived for web gaming, WebAssembly has broader applications.

Benefits of WebAssembly

- **Performance:** WebAssembly allows developers to run computationally intensive tasks with near-native performance.

- **Language Agnostic:** You can write code in languages like C, C++, Rust, and even Python, and compile them to WebAssembly.

- **Browser Compatibility:** It's supported across all major browsers, making it a universal technology.

Using WebAssembly in Front-End Development

Here's a simple example of using WebAssembly to perform a computationally intensive task in a web application:

1. Write WebAssembly Code (e.g., in C++):

```c
// factorial.c
int factorial(int n) {
  if (n <= 1) return 1;
  return n * factorial(n - 1);
}
```

2. Compile to WebAssembly:

```bash
emcc -o factorial.wasm factorial.c
```

3. Use WebAssembly in JavaScript:

```javascript
fetch('factorial.wasm')
  .then(response => response.arrayBuffer())
  .then(bytes => WebAssembly.instantiate(bytes, {}))
```

```
 .then(results => {

   const exports = results.instance.exports;

   const result = exports.factorial(5);

   console.log(result); // Output: 120

 });
```
```

This example demonstrates how WebAssembly can be used to offload CPU-intensive tasks to the browser, enhancing the user experience.

## Machine Learning in the Browser

### Introduction to In-Browser Machine Learning

Machine learning (ML) and artificial intelligence (AI) are increasingly making their way into front-end development. With technologies like TensorFlow.js and ONNX.js, developers can run machine learning models directly in the browser.

### Benefits of In-Browser ML

- **Low Latency**: Running ML models in the browser reduces the need for server round trips, leading to lower latency.

- **Privacy:** Sensitive data can stay on the client-side, improving user privacy.

- **Offline Capabilities:** ML models can run even when the user is offline.
```

Using In-Browser Machine Learning

Here's a simplified example of using TensorFlow.js to perform image classification in the browser:

```javascript
// Load a pre-trained model
const model = await tf.loadLayersModel('model.json');

// Get an image from the DOM
const img = document.getElementById('image');

// Preprocess the image (e.g., resize and normalize)

// Make predictions
const predictions = await model.predict(preprocessedImage);

// Display the results
console.log(predictions);
```

This showcases how machine learning can enhance user experiences in web applications, from image recognition to natural language processing.

Focus on Accessibility and Inclusivity

Continued Emphasis on Accessibility

As web applications become more complex, there is a growing emphasis on ensuring they are accessible to all users, including those with disabilities. Compliance with accessibility standards like WCAG (Web Content Accessibility Guidelines) will be a standard practice.

AI-Driven Accessibility

Artificial intelligence and machine learning will play a role in making web applications more accessible. For example, AI-driven tools can automatically generate alt text for images or suggest improvements to accessibility.

Conclusion

The future of front-end development promises exciting advancements. WebAssembly brings high-performance computing to the browser, in-browser machine learning opens up new possibilities, and accessibility continues to be a top priority. Embracing these trends will empower front-end developers to create faster, smarter, and more inclusive web applications.

CHAPTER XII
Building a Portfolio and Showcasing Your Work

12.1 Creating a Professional Portfolio

In today's competitive job market, having a professional portfolio is essential for front-end developers. It's not just a collection of your work; it's your showcase to the world. In this section, we'll guide you through the process of creating a compelling portfolio step by step.

Step 1: Define Your Goals

Before diving into creating your portfolio, it's essential to define your goals. Consider what you want to achieve with your portfolio:

- Are you looking for a job?

- Do you want to attract freelance clients?

- Are you aiming to showcase your skills to potential collaborators?

Your goals will influence the content and structure of your portfolio.

Step 2: Select Your Best Work

Quality over quantity is the key here. Choose a selection of your best projects to showcase. Ideally, you should have a mix of personal projects, freelance work, and any contributions to open-source projects.

Step 3: Design a Clean and User-Friendly Layout

Your portfolio's design should be clean and easy to navigate. A cluttered or confusing layout can turn visitors away. Here are some design principles to keep in mind:

- **Simplicity:** Keep it simple and avoid unnecessary elements.

- **Navigation:** Make it easy for visitors to find their way around your portfolio.

- **Responsive Design:** Ensure your portfolio is mobile-friendly.

- **Consistency:** Maintain a consistent color scheme and typography.

Step 4: Showcase Your Work

For each project, provide the following details:

- **Project Title:** A clear and concise title.

- **Description:** Describe the project's purpose, your role, and the technologies used.

- **Screenshots:** Include screenshots or images of the project.

- **Links:** Add links to live demos or GitHub repositories.

- **Technologies:** List the technologies and tools used.

Step 5: About Me Section

Include an "About Me" section where you can introduce yourself, your background, and your passion for front-end development. This section helps potential employers or clients get to know you better.

Step 6: Contact Information

Make sure visitors can easily contact you. Include your email address, LinkedIn profile, and any other relevant contact information.

Step 7: Testimonials and References

If you have received positive feedback or worked with clients or collaborators who can vouch for your skills, consider including testimonials or references.

Step 8: Blog or Articles (Optional)

If you enjoy writing about web development, consider adding a blog section to your portfolio. Sharing your knowledge can showcase your expertise and attract a broader audience.

Step 9: Regularly Update Your Portfolio

Your portfolio is a dynamic representation of your skills and growth. Make a habit of updating it regularly with new projects and skills you've acquired.

Step 10: Get Feedback

Before finalizing your portfolio, ask for feedback from peers, mentors, or colleagues. Fresh eyes can provide valuable insights and help you identify areas for improvement.

Conclusion

A professional portfolio is your passport to opportunities in front-end development. By following these steps and continuously improving your portfolio, you can effectively showcase your skills and stand out in the competitive world of web development.

12.2 Version Control and Code Hosting

In the world of web development, version control and code hosting are essential tools for managing your projects efficiently and collaborating with others. In this section, we'll explore how to use version control systems like Git and host your code on platforms like GitHub.

Introduction to Version Control

Version control is a system that helps you manage changes to your codebase over time. It tracks modifications, enables collaboration, and provides a safety net for your projects. Git is the most widely used version control system in the web development community.

Getting Started with Git

Step 1: Installing Git

Before you can start using Git, you need to install it on your computer. You can download Git from the official website (https://git-scm.com/downloads) and follow the installation instructions for your specific operating system.

Step 2: Configuration

After installation, configure Git with your name and email address using the following commands:

```bash
```

git config --global user.name "Your Name"

git config --global user.email "youremail@example.com"

```

## Step 3: Creating a Git Repository

To start tracking changes in a project, navigate to your project's directory and initialize a Git repository:

```bash
cd your-project-directory

git init
```

Step 4: Adding Files

Use the `git add` command to stage files for a commit. For example, to stage a file named "index.html," run:

```bash
git add index.html
```

Step 5: Making Commits
```

Create a commit to save your staged changes:

```bash
git commit -m "Your commit message here"
```

Step 6: Viewing History

You can view the commit history using:

```bash
git log
```

Collaboration with GitHub

GitHub is a popular platform for hosting Git repositories and collaborating with others. Here's how to get started with GitHub:

Step 1: Sign Up for GitHub

If you don't have a GitHub account, sign up at https://github.com/.

Step 2: Creating a Repository

Click the "New" button on your GitHub dashboard to create a new repository. You can choose to make it public or private.

Step 3: Pushing Code to GitHub

To push your local Git repository to GitHub, use the following commands:

```bash
git remote add origin https://github.com/yourusername/your-repo.git
git branch -M main
git push -u origin main
```

Replace `yourusername` with your GitHub username and `your-repo` with your repository name.

Collaborative Workflows

GitHub allows you to collaborate with others using features like pull requests, issues, and project boards. Here's a basic collaborative workflow:

1. Clone a repository: Use `git clone` to create a local copy of a GitHub repository on your computer.

2. Create a branch: Use `git checkout -b new-branch` to create a new branch for your work.

3. Make changes: Edit your code as needed.

4. Commit changes: Use `git add` and `git commit` to save your changes.

5. Push changes: Push your branch to GitHub using `git push origin new-branch`.

6. Create a pull request: On GitHub, create a pull request to merge your changes into the main branch.

7. Review and merge: Collaborators can review your code and merge it if it's approved.

Conclusion

Version control with Git and code hosting on platforms like GitHub are indispensable skills for modern web developers. They facilitate collaboration, provide a safety net for your projects, and help you showcase your work to potential employers or clients. By following these steps, you'll be well on your way to mastering these essential tools.

12.3 Personal Branding and Networking

In today's competitive job market, personal branding and networking are crucial for advancing your career as a web developer. In this section, we'll explore how to build a strong personal brand, create an online presence, and establish valuable professional connections.

The Importance of Personal Branding

Your personal brand is how you present yourself to the world, both online and offline. It encompasses your skills, values, personality, and what you're known for. Effective personal branding can help you stand out from the crowd and attract the right opportunities.

Building Your Personal Brand

Step 1: Self-Reflection

Start by identifying your strengths, weaknesses, passions, and values. What sets you apart from other developers? Understanding your unique qualities is the foundation of your personal brand.

Step 2: Define Your Niche

Consider specializing in a particular area of web development that aligns with your interests and expertise. Whether it's front-end development, back-end development, UX/UI design, or a specific technology stack, being a specialist can make you more memorable.

Step 3: Create an Online Presence

1. Professional Website: Build a personal website or portfolio to showcase your work, projects, and skills. Use your real name as the domain (e.g., www.yourname.com).

2. Blog/Vlog: Share your knowledge and insights by writing blog posts or creating videos on platforms like Medium, Dev.to, or YouTube.

3. Social Media: Use LinkedIn, Twitter, and other social platforms to share industry-related content, engage with others, and demonstrate your expertise.

4. GitHub: Maintain an active GitHub profile to showcase your coding skills and contributions to open-source projects.

Step 4: Consistent Branding

Ensure that your branding elements, such as your website, resume, social profiles, and business cards, have a consistent visual identity, including colors, fonts, and logos.

Networking Strategies

Step 5: Attend Events

Participate in web development meetups, conferences, and workshops. These events provide opportunities to meet industry professionals, learn from experts, and expand your network.

Step 6: Join Online Communities

Engage with web development communities on platforms like GitHub, Stack Overflow, Reddit, and relevant forums. Answer questions, seek advice, and share your knowledge.

Step 7: Mentorship

Consider both mentoring others and seeking mentors. Mentorship relationships can offer guidance, insights, and access to valuable connections.

Step 8: Cold Outreach

Don't hesitate to reach out to professionals or companies you admire. Craft personalized messages explaining your interest and how you believe you can add value.

Maintaining Your Network

Step 9: Follow Up

After meeting new contacts, follow up with a thank-you message and stay in touch periodically. Networking is an ongoing process, not a one-time event.

Step 10: Provide Value

Actively look for opportunities to help others in your network. Whether it's sharing a job posting, providing feedback, or offering assistance, generosity goes a long way.

Conclusion

Personal branding and networking are integral components of a successful career in web development. By building a strong personal brand and nurturing meaningful connections within the industry, you'll increase your chances of landing exciting job opportunities, collaborating on interesting projects, and advancing your career to new heights. Remember that authenticity and genuine engagement are key to establishing a positive and influential online presence.

12.4 Preparing for Interviews and Job Searches

Landing your dream job as a web developer requires more than just technical skills. It involves a strategic approach to job searching, preparing for interviews, and effectively showcasing your qualifications. In this section, we will delve into the steps you can take to maximize your chances of success in the job market.

Step 1: Self-Assessment

Before you start your job search, take some time for self-assessment. Understand your career goals, preferences, and the type of work culture that suits you best. This will help you target the right positions and companies.

Step 2: Resume Building

A compelling resume is your ticket to getting noticed by potential employers. Here's how to create an effective one:

Structuring Your Resume

1. Contact Information: Include your name, phone number, email, and a link to your professional website or LinkedIn profile.

2. Summary/Objective: Write a brief summary highlighting your skills and career goals.

3. Skills: List your technical skills, including programming languages, frameworks, and tools you are proficient in.

4. Experience: Detail your work experience, emphasizing your achievements and contributions to previous employers. Use quantifiable results whenever possible.

5. Projects: Highlight significant projects you've worked on, including your role, technologies used, and outcomes.

6. Education: Mention your educational background, including degrees, institutions, and graduation dates.

Tailoring Your Resume

Customize your resume for each job application. Focus on the skills and experiences that are most relevant to the position you're applying for.

Step 3: Online Presence

Maintain a professional online presence:

LinkedIn

1. Create or update your LinkedIn profile, emphasizing your skills, experiences, and projects.

2. Connect with industry professionals and follow companies you're interested in.

3. Share relevant content and engage in discussions to demonstrate your expertise.

GitHub

1. Keep your GitHub profile active by contributing to open-source projects or working on personal projects.

2. Showcase your coding skills and commitment to the field.

Step 4: Job Search

Job Boards

Use job boards like LinkedIn, Indeed, Glassdoor, and specialized tech job boards to find relevant positions.

Company Websites

Explore the career pages of companies you admire. Many companies post job openings on their websites before listing them on job boards.

Networking

Leverage your network to uncover hidden job opportunities. Attend meetups, conferences, and online events to connect with professionals in the industry.

Step 5: Interview Preparation

Successful interviews require thorough preparation:

Research

1. Research the company's history, culture, values, and products or services.

2. Understand the job description and requirements thoroughly.

Behavioral Questions

Prepare answers to common behavioral questions using the STAR (Situation, Task, Action, Result) method.

Technical Questions

Review technical concepts and practice coding problems related to the position you're applying for.

Mock Interviews

Conduct mock interviews with friends or mentors to practice your responses and improve your confidence.

Step 6: Portfolio Presentation

Be ready to showcase your work:

Online Portfolio

Ensure your online portfolio is up to date with your latest projects, descriptions, and links to live demos or code repositories.

Project Walkthroughs

Practice explaining your projects concisely and compellingly, emphasizing the technical challenges you overcame.

Step 7: The Interview

On the day of the interview:

Dress Professionally

Wear appropriate attire for the type of company and position you're interviewing for.

Be Punctual

Arrive early for in-person interviews or log in on time for virtual interviews.

Follow Up

Send a thank-you email after the interview to express your gratitude and reiterate your interest in the position.

Step 8: Salary Negotiation

If you receive an offer, don't be afraid to negotiate your salary and benefits. Research industry standards and be prepared to make a counteroffer if necessary.

Conclusion

Preparing for interviews and job searches is a systematic process that requires careful planning and execution. By following these steps, you can position yourself as a strong candidate in the competitive world of web development and increase your chances of securing the job you desire. Remember that continuous learning, networking, and a positive attitude can go a long way in your career journey.

CHAPTER XIII
Conclusion and Looking Ahead

13.1 Recap of Front-End Techniques

As we come to the conclusion of this guide on front-end development, it's essential to recap the key front-end techniques and concepts we've covered throughout the book. These techniques form the foundation of modern web development and will continue to be relevant as the field evolves.

HTML

HTML (Hypertext Markup Language) is the backbone of web content. Some essential HTML concepts to remember:

1. Semantic HTML: Use semantic elements like `<header>`, `<nav>`, `<main>`, and `<footer>` to structure your content logically, improving accessibility and SEO.

2. Forms: Create interactive forms using `<form>`, `<input>`, and other form elements. Implement client-side validation for user-friendly experiences.

CSS

CSS (Cascading Style Sheets) is used for styling and layout. Key CSS concepts include:

1. Selectors: Target HTML elements using selectors like class, ID, and element selectors.

2. Box Model: Understand how the box model affects element sizing and spacing.

3. Flexbox and Grid: Master layout techniques using Flexbox and Grid for responsive designs.

4. CSS Preprocessors: Explore CSS preprocessors like Sass or Less for efficient and organized stylesheets.

JavaScript

JavaScript is the language of interactivity and dynamic web content. Important JavaScript concepts include:

1. Variables and Data Types: Learn how to declare variables and work with different data types like strings, numbers, and objects.

2. Functions: Write reusable code blocks using functions, and understand function expressions and arrow functions.

3. DOM Manipulation: Access and manipulate the Document Object Model (DOM) to update web content dynamically.

4. Event Handling: Respond to user interactions with event listeners and handlers.

5. AJAX and Fetch API: Communicate with servers asynchronously to fetch and send data.

Responsive Design

Create web applications that adapt to various screen sizes and devices. Key responsive design principles include:

1. Media Queries: Use media queries to apply different styles based on screen size.

2. Viewport Meta Tag: Include the viewport meta tag to control the initial scaling of web pages on mobile devices.

3. Fluid Layouts: Design layouts with flexible units like percentages to ensure responsiveness.

Performance Optimization

Improve web page performance for a better user experience. Techniques for optimization include:

1. Minification: Minify HTML, CSS, and JavaScript files to reduce file sizes.

2. Image Optimization: Compress and serve images in modern formats like WebP.

3. Lazy Loading: Delay loading off-screen images and resources until they're needed.

4. Code Splitting: Split JavaScript bundles to load only the necessary code for each page.

Accessibility

Ensure that your web applications are accessible to all users, including those with disabilities. Some accessibility best practices:

1. Semantic HTML: Use semantic HTML elements for meaningful page structure.

2. Alt Text: Provide descriptive alt text for images.

3. Keyboard Navigation: Ensure that all interactive elements are accessible via keyboard.

4. ARIA: Implement ARIA roles and attributes for complex widgets.

5. Testing: Regularly test your website with screen readers and accessibility tools.

These are the fundamental front-end techniques that every web developer should be familiar with. However, remember that the web development landscape is constantly evolving, and staying up-to-date with new technologies and best practices is essential for continued success in this field. In the next sections, we'll discuss the importance of embracing continuous learning and explore the future of front-end development.

13.2 Embracing Continuous Learning

In the ever-evolving field of front-end development, the journey doesn't end with the completion of this guide. Embracing continuous learning is a critical mindset for any web developer. Here, we'll explore strategies and resources to help you stay current and continually improve your skills.

1. Stay Updated with Web Standards and Technologies

Web technologies are constantly evolving. Keep yourself updated with the latest HTML, CSS, and JavaScript specifications. Subscribe to newsletters, follow blogs, and join online communities where experts discuss emerging standards and best practices.

2. Learn from Open Source Projects

Contributing to open-source projects is an excellent way to learn from experienced developers, collaborate with others, and give back to the community. GitHub is a great platform to find open-source projects related to front-end development.

3. Online Courses and Tutorials

Platforms like Coursera, edX, Udemy, and freeCodeCamp offer a wide range of online courses and tutorials covering various aspects of front-end development. These courses often include hands-on exercises and projects to practice your skills.

4. Read Documentation and Documentation-Like Code

Exploring the official documentation of libraries, frameworks, and tools is essential. Documentation provides in-depth information, examples, and best practices. Reading code from well-established open-source projects can also be educational.

5. Follow Industry Leaders on Social Media

Follow front-end experts, developers, and thought leaders on platforms like Twitter, LinkedIn, and Dev.to. They often share valuable insights, tutorials, and news about the industry.

6. Build Personal Projects

Practical experience is one of the most effective ways to learn. Challenge yourself by building personal projects that interest you. Whether it's a portfolio website, a web app, or a simple widget, hands-on practice is invaluable.

7. Attend Conferences and Meetups

Front-end development conferences and meetups provide opportunities to network with peers, attend talks by industry leaders, and gain inspiration from real-world projects. Many events offer online options, making them accessible worldwide.

8. Experiment with New Technologies

Don't be afraid to experiment with new technologies, libraries, and frameworks. Create small projects to test new concepts, and consider how they might improve your workflow or enhance your projects.

9. Seek Feedback and Collaboration

Share your work with others and seek feedback. Collaboration with fellow developers can lead to valuable insights and mentorship opportunities. Don't hesitate to ask questions and engage with the developer community.

10. Stay Informed About Accessibility and Inclusivity

As web accessibility standards evolve, staying informed about accessible design and development is crucial. Continue learning about WCAG guidelines and inclusive design principles to create web experiences that are accessible to all users.

Remember that learning in the tech industry is a continuous journey. No matter your level of expertise, there is always something new to explore and discover. Front-end development is a dynamic field, and by embracing continuous learning, you'll be well-prepared to adapt to future challenges and opportunities.

13.3 Front-End Development in an Evolving Web Landscape

Front-end development is a dynamic and ever-evolving field. As we conclude this guide, it's essential to look ahead and understand how the landscape of web development is changing. In this section, we'll explore the key trends and areas to focus on for staying relevant in the industry.

1. Responsive and Mobile-First Design

Mobile internet usage continues to grow, emphasizing the importance of responsive and mobile-first design. Ensure that your websites and applications are optimized for various devices and screen sizes. Consider using CSS frameworks like Bootstrap or responsive design techniques such as Flexbox and Grid.

2. Web Performance and Speed

Web users have high expectations for speed and performance. Google's Core Web Vitals and other performance metrics play a crucial role in SEO and user experience. Optimize your code, utilize efficient asset loading techniques, and consider progressive web app (PWA) principles to improve website performance.

3. PWA and Offline Support

Progressive Web Apps (PWAs) offer users a native app-like experience in the web browser. PWAs work offline, load quickly, and can be installed on users' devices. Learning to develop PWAs can give your projects a competitive edge.

4. WebAssembly (Wasm)

WebAssembly is changing the game by allowing high-performance, low-level languages like C++ and Rust to run in web browsers. Explore the potential of WebAssembly for tasks that require significant computational power or real-time performance.

5. Serverless Architecture

Serverless computing allows developers to build and run applications without managing servers. Platforms like AWS Lambda and Azure Functions simplify backend development, enabling you to focus more on front-end features.

6. JAMstack Architecture

The JAMstack architecture (JavaScript, APIs, and Markup) decouples the front end from the backend, making websites faster, more secure, and easier to scale. Learning how to build JAMstack applications with technologies like Gatsby or Next.js can be advantageous.

7. Accessibility and Inclusivity

Web accessibility isn't just a trend; it's a fundamental requirement. Stay up to date with accessibility guidelines and best practices to ensure that your web projects are inclusive and accessible to all users, regardless of their abilities.

8. AI and Machine Learning Integration

AI and machine learning are being integrated into web applications for tasks like personalization, content recommendation, and chatbots. Familiarize yourself with AI and ML concepts to stay relevant in this evolving landscape.

9. Static Site Generators

Static site generators (SSGs) are gaining popularity for their simplicity and performance benefits. Explore SSGs like Hugo, Jekyll, or Eleventy for building fast and secure websites.

10. Ethical and Sustainable Web Development

Consider the environmental impact of web development. Optimize your code, reduce unnecessary energy consumption, and support sustainable hosting solutions to create a more eco-friendly web.

As a front-end developer, adaptability and a willingness to learn new technologies and techniques are key to success in this evolving landscape. Stay curious, keep experimenting, and be open to change. The web development journey is a dynamic one, and by staying informed and proactive, you'll continue to thrive in this ever-changing field.

Appendix A
HTML and CSS Reference

HTML Elements and Attributes

This appendix serves as a quick reference guide for HTML elements and attributes. HTML (Hypertext Markup Language) is the foundation of web development, used to structure web content. Understanding the different elements and attributes at your disposal is essential for creating well-structured web pages.

1. HTML Elements

HTML elements define the structure and content of a web page. Here are some common HTML elements:

`<html>`

The root element that encloses all other HTML elements on the page.

```html
<!DOCTYPE html>
<html>
  <!-- The rest of your HTML content goes here -->
```

```
</html>
```

`<head>`

Contains metadata about the document, such as the page title and links to external resources.

```html
<head>
  <title>My Web Page</title>
  <link rel="stylesheet" href="styles.css">
</head>
```

`<body>`

Encloses the visible content of the web page, including text, images, and other elements.

```html
<body>
  <h1>Welcome to My Web Page</h1>
  <p>This is a sample paragraph.</p>
  <img src="image.jpg" alt="A sample image">
</body>
```

`<div>`

A generic container used for grouping and styling elements.

```html
<div class="container">
  <p>This is a div element.</p>
</div>
```

`<a>`

Creates hyperlinks to other web pages or resources.

```html
<a href="https://www.example.com">Visit Example.com</a>
```

2. HTML Attributes

HTML attributes provide additional information about elements and how they should behave. Here are some commonly used HTML attributes:

`id`

Assigns a unique identifier to an element, often used for JavaScript and CSS styling.

```html
<div id="myDiv">This div has an ID.</div>
```

`class`

Assigns one or more class names to an element, used for CSS styling and JavaScript targeting.

```html
<p class="important-text">This text is important.</p>
```

`src`

Specifies the source URL for elements like images and iframes.

```html
<img src="image.jpg" alt="A sample image">
```

`href`

Specifies the destination URL for anchor (`<a>`) elements.

```html
<a href="https://www.example.com">Visit Example.com</a>
```

`alt`

Provides alternative text for images, which is important for accessibility.

```html
<img src="image.jpg" alt="A descriptive image caption">
```

`style`

Inline CSS styles that can be applied directly to an element.

```html
<p style="color: blue; font-size: 16px;">Styled paragraph text.</p>
```

`target`

Determines how links should open. "_blank" opens the link in a new tab.

```html
<a href="https://www.example.com" target="_blank">Visit Example.com</a>
```

`rel`

Specifies the relationship between the current document and a linked resource.

```html
<link rel="stylesheet" href="styles.css">
```

This reference provides a glimpse into HTML elements and attributes. As you continue your journey in web development, you'll explore more elements and attributes and learn how to use them effectively to create engaging and accessible web content.

Common CSS Properties and Values

In this section, we'll delve into common CSS (Cascading Style Sheets) properties and values. CSS is essential for styling web pages, allowing you to control the layout, appearance, and presentation of your HTML content. Understanding these properties and values is crucial for effective web design.

Here are some frequently used CSS properties and their associated values:

`color`

The `color` property sets the text color of an element. It can accept color values in various formats, such as named colors, hexadecimal codes, RGB, or HSL values.

```css
/* Using a named color */
p {
  color: red;
}

/* Using a hexadecimal code */
h1 {
  color: #00aabb;
}
```

```css
/* Using RGB values */
a {
  color: rgb(255, 100, 0);
}


/* Using HSL values */
button {
  color: hsl(120, 100%, 50%);
}
```

`font-size`

`font-size` determines the size of text within an element. You can specify it in pixels, em units, percentages, or other valid length units.

```css
p {
  font-size: 16px;
}


h1 {
  font-size: 2em;
}
```

```
```

`font-family`

This property sets the font family for text content. It allows you to specify a prioritized list of font choices.

```css
body {
  font-family: Arial, Helvetica, sans-serif;
}
```

`background-color`

`background-color` defines the background color of an element. Like the `color` property, it accepts various color value formats.

```css
section {
  background-color: #f0f0f0;
}
```

`margin` and `padding`

`margin` controls the space outside an element, while `padding` manages the space inside. They can take multiple values to specify margins/padding for different sides (top, right, bottom, left).

```css
div {
  margin: 10px; /* Applies to all sides */
  padding: 20px 10px; /* Vertical and horizontal values */
  /* padding: 10px 20px 15px 5px; Top, right, bottom, left */
}
```

`border`

The `border` property allows you to set borders around elements. It includes properties like `border-width`, `border-style`, and `border-color`.

```css
button {
  border: 2px solid #333; /* 2px solid border with color */
}
```

`width` and `height`

These properties define the width and height of elements. They can accept values in pixels, percentages, or other valid length units.

```css
img {
  width: 100%;
  height: auto; /* Maintains aspect ratio */
}
```

`display`

`display` determines how an element should be displayed on the page. Common values include `block`, `inline`, and `flex`.

```css
ul {
  display: inline; /* Renders as an inline element */
}
```

`text-align`

`text-align` controls the horizontal alignment of text content within an element.

```css
h2 {
  text-align: center; /* Centers text horizontally */
}
```

`position` and `top`, `right`, `bottom`, `left`

These properties are used for CSS positioning. `position` defines the positioning type (e.g., `relative`, `absolute`), while the others adjust the element's position within its container.

```css
div {
  position: relative; /* Relative to its normal position */
  top: 10px;
  left: 20px;
}
```

These are just a few examples of common CSS properties and values. CSS offers a wide range of properties for creating stunning web designs. As you gain experience in front-end development, you'll explore more CSS properties and develop a deeper understanding of how to style your web pages effectively.

Appendix B
JavaScript Reference

JavaScript Objects and Methods

In this section, we'll explore common JavaScript objects and methods that are essential for front-end development. JavaScript is a versatile programming language that allows you to add interactivity and dynamic behavior to web pages. Understanding these objects and methods is crucial for effective front-end development.

`document`

The `document` object represents the HTML document in the browser. It provides methods to interact with the DOM (Document Object Model) and manipulate the content of web pages.

Example: Accessing Elements by ID

```javascript
// Access an element by its ID
const heading = document.getElementById('my-heading');
```

`window`

The `window` object represents the browser window or tab. It provides methods and properties for controlling the browser, handling events, and managing cookies.

Example: Opening a New Browser Window

```javascript
// Open a new browser window
const newWindow = window.open('https://example.com', '_blank');
```

`String`

The `String` object represents a sequence of characters. It provides various methods for working with strings, such as concatenation, substring extraction, and searching.

Example: String Concatenation

```javascript
const firstName = 'John';
const lastName = 'Doe';
const fullName = firstName + ' ' + lastName;
```

`Array`

The `Array` object represents a collection of elements. It provides methods for adding, removing, and manipulating elements within an array.

Example: Adding and Removing Elements from an Array

```javascript
const fruits = ['apple', 'banana', 'cherry'];
fruits.push('orange'); // Add an element to the end
fruits.pop(); // Remove the last element
```

`Event`

The `Event` object represents an event that occurs in the DOM, such as a mouse click or keyboard press. It contains information about the event and methods for handling it.

Example: Event Handling

```javascript
const button = document.getElementById('my-button');
button.addEventListener('click', function(event) {
  alert('Button clicked!');
});
```

`XMLHttpRequest` (XHR)

The `XMLHttpRequest` object is used for making HTTP requests from JavaScript. It allows you to fetch data from a server without requiring a page reload.

Example: Making an AJAX Request

```javascript
const xhr = new XMLHttpRequest();
xhr.open('GET', 'https://api.example.com/data', true);
xhr.onreadystatechange = function() {
  if (xhr.readyState === 4 && xhr.status === 200) {
    const response = JSON.parse(xhr.responseText);
    console.log(response);
  }
};
xhr.send();
```

`fetch()`

The `fetch()` method is a modern alternative to `XMLHttpRequest` for making HTTP requests. It returns a Promise and simplifies data retrieval and handling.

Example: Fetching Data with `fetch()`

```javascript
fetch('https://api.example.com/data')

  .then(response => response.json())

  .then(data => console.log(data))

  .catch(error => console.error('Error:', error));

```

These are just a few examples of JavaScript objects and methods commonly used in front-end development. JavaScript offers a vast ecosystem of libraries and frameworks that can further enhance your web development capabilities. As you continue to explore JavaScript, you'll discover more objects and methods to help you create interactive and dynamic web applications.

Common JavaScript Events

In this section, we will delve into common JavaScript events that play a pivotal role in front-end web development. JavaScript events allow you to respond to user interactions and trigger specific actions within your web applications.

JavaScript events are occurrences that take place while a user interacts with a web page. Event handling is crucial for creating responsive and interactive web applications. Here are some common JavaScript events and how to use them:

1. Click Event

The `click` event is triggered when an element, such as a button or a link, is clicked by the user.

Example: Handling a Click Event

```javascript
const button = document.getElementById('my-button');
button.addEventListener('click', function(event) {
  // Code to execute when the button is clicked
  alert('Button clicked!');
});
```

2. Mouseover and Mouseout Events

The `mouseover` event occurs when the user's mouse pointer enters an element, while the `mouseout` event occurs when the mouse pointer exits the element.

Example: Responding to Mouseover and Mouseout

```javascript
const element = document.getElementById('my-element');
element.addEventListener('mouseover', function(event) {
  // Code to execute when the mouse enters the element
  element.style.backgroundColor = 'lightblue';
});

element.addEventListener('mouseout', function(event) {
  // Code to execute when the mouse leaves the element
  element.style.backgroundColor = 'white';
});
```

3. Keydown and Keypress Events

The `keydown` event is triggered when a key is pressed down, and the `keypress` event is triggered when a key is pressed and released.

Example: Handling Key Events

```javascript
document.addEventListener('keydown', function(event) {
  // Check if the 'Enter' key is pressed
  if (event.key === 'Enter') {
    // Code to execute when 'Enter' key is pressed
    alert('Enter key pressed!');
  }
});
```

4. Submit Event

The `submit` event is fired when a form is submitted, typically by clicking a submit button.

Example: Handling a Form Submission

```javascript
const form = document.getElementById('my-form');
form.addEventListener('submit', function(event) {
  // Prevent the default form submission behavior
  event.preventDefault();
```

```
// Code to handle form submission
const formData = new FormData(form);
// Perform form data processing
});
```

5. Resize Event

The `resize` event is triggered when the browser window is resized.

Example: Responding to Window Resize

```javascript
window.addEventListener('resize', function(event) {
  // Code to execute when the window is resized
  console.log('Window resized!');
});
```

6. Load Event

The `load` event is fired when a web page or external resource (e.g., an image) finishes loading.

Example: Handling Page Load

```javascript
window.addEventListener('load', function(event) {
  // Code to execute when the page has fully loaded
  console.log('Page loaded!');
});
```

These are just a few examples of common JavaScript events that you may encounter in front-end development. Understanding how to use events and event listeners is essential for creating dynamic and interactive web applications. As you work on your projects, you'll discover even more events and opportunities to enhance user interactions on your web pages.

Glossary

Key Terms and Definitions

In this glossary section, we will define key terms and concepts commonly used in front-end development. Understanding these terms is essential for effectively working in the field of web development.

Key Terms and Definitions

1. HTML (Hypertext Markup Language)

HTML is the standard markup language used for creating web pages. It defines the structure and content of a web page using elements and tags. For example:

```html
<!DOCTYPE html>
<html>
  <head>
    <title>My Web Page</title>
  </head>
  <body>
    <h1>Welcome to My Web Page</h1>
```

```
  <p>This is a paragraph of text.</p>

 </body>

</html>

```

2. CSS (Cascading Style Sheets)

CSS is a stylesheet language used for describing the presentation and layout of web pages. It is used to style HTML elements. For example:

```css
/* CSS code to style a paragraph */

p {

  color: blue;

  font-size: 16px;

}

```

3. JavaScript

JavaScript is a versatile programming language that allows you to add interactivity and functionality to web pages. It can be used for tasks like form validation, DOM manipulation, and creating interactive features.

```javascript
```

```javascript
// JavaScript code to display an alert
alert('Hello, World!');
```

4. DOM (Document Object Model)

The DOM is a programming interface for web documents. It represents the page so that programs can change the document structure, style, and content dynamically. For example, you can use JavaScript to modify the DOM:

```javascript
// JavaScript code to change the text of an element
const element = document.getElementById('my-element');
element.textContent = 'New Text';
```

5. Responsive Design

Responsive design is an approach to web design that makes web pages render well on a variety of devices and window sizes. It uses CSS techniques like media queries to adjust the layout and styling.

```css
/* CSS code for a responsive layout */
@media screen and (max-width: 600px) {
```

```
/* Styles for small screens */
body {
  font-size: 14px;
  }
}
```

6. API (Application Programming Interface)

An API is a set of rules and protocols that allows different software applications to communicate with each other. Web APIs, in particular, allow web services and applications to interact.

```javascript
// Using a web API to fetch data
fetch('https://api.example.com/data')
  .then(response => response.json())
  .then(data => console.log(data));
```

7. Front-End Frameworks

Front-end frameworks, like React, Angular, and Vue.js, provide pre-built components and a structured approach to building user interfaces. They simplify and speed up front-end development.

```javascript
// Example of using React to create a component
import React from 'react';


function App() {
  return <div>Hello, World!</div>;
}


export default App;
```

8. Single-Page Application (SPA)

An SPA is a web application or website that interacts with the user dynamically by rewriting the current page rather than loading entire new pages from the server. It offers a smoother user experience.

9. Web Accessibility

Web accessibility refers to designing and developing websites and applications that can be used by people with disabilities. It involves providing alternative text for images, keyboard navigation, and other features.

10. Progressive Web App (PWA)

A PWA is a web application that uses modern web technologies to provide an app-like experience to users. PWAs can work offline and offer features like push notifications.

These are some of the key terms and definitions that you may encounter in front-end development. Familiarizing yourself with these concepts is crucial for success in the field, and as you continue your journey, you'll encounter more specialized terminology related to specific technologies and trends.

Conclusion

As we conclude this comprehensive guide to front-end development, we want to extend our heartfelt gratitude to you, the reader, for embarking on this learning journey with us. Front-end development is an ever-evolving field that plays a pivotal role in shaping the web landscape, and your dedication to honing your skills in this domain is commendable.

Throughout this book, we've explored a wide array of topics, ranging from the foundational principles of HTML, CSS, and JavaScript to the intricacies of modern web development, including responsive design, front-end frameworks, web accessibility, and emerging trends. We've provided detailed explanations, practical examples, and best practices to empower you with the knowledge and skills needed to excel in front-end development.

As you reflect on your journey through these pages, remember that the world of web development is dynamic, and continuous learning is key to staying relevant and thriving in this industry. The technologies and tools we've covered are just the tip of the iceberg, and there's always something new to discover and master.

Embrace continuous learning as a lifelong commitment. Follow industry trends, explore emerging technologies, and contribute to the vibrant developer community. Leverage online resources, attend meetups, and consider participating in open-source projects to enhance your skills and broaden your horizons.

Front-end development is not just about creating beautiful and functional user interfaces; it's about crafting digital experiences that resonate with users and make a positive impact on the web. Your dedication to this craft can lead to exciting career opportunities, innovative projects, and the satisfaction of contributing to the ever-evolving web landscape.

As you move forward in your journey, remember that the skills you've acquired here are not just tools for building websites; they are instruments for bringing your creative visions to life and making a meaningful mark on the digital world.

Thank you once again for choosing this book as your companion on your front-end development journey. We wish you continued success, creativity, and fulfillment in your endeavors. The future of front-end development is bright, and we can't wait to see the incredible contributions you'll make to the web. Happy coding!

www.ingramcontent.com/pod-product-compliance
Lightning Source LLC
Chambersburg PA
CBHW080357060326
40689CB00019B/4039